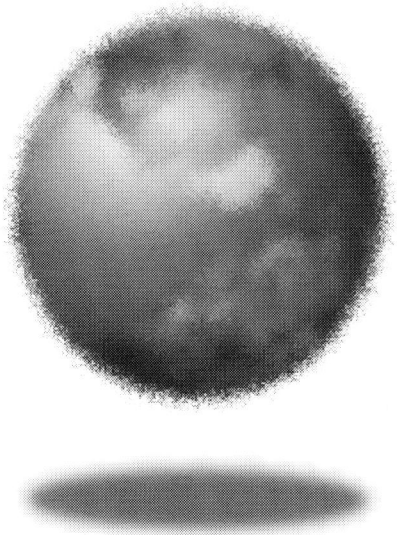

"Feminism means the action by women and men to establish equality and justice for women. It is, in fact, the only female gendered word in the English language that includes both women and men."

—Florence Howe, Director and Publisher

The Feminist Press at The City University of New York

1

Library of Congress Cataloging-in-Publication Data

Re-visioning feminism around the world.
            p.   cm.
      ISBN 1-55861-114-2
            1.Feminism——History. 2. Feminist theory——
United States. 3. Feminism—United States—History. 4. Femi-
nist theory——United States. 5. Feminist Press——History.
I. Feminist Press.
HQ1154.R45 1995
305.42——dc20   95-5135
                                                      CIP

*The Feminist Press at CUNY wishes to acknowledge the
generous support of the AT&T Foundation and its help
in the preparation and publication of this volume.*

RE-VISIONING FEMINISM AROUND THE WORLD

THE FEMINIST PRESS AT THE CITY UNIVERSITY OF NEW YORK
NEW YORK

3

TABLE OF CONTENTS

Here's to the Next Twenty-Five

Florence Howe

FIFTEEN YEARS AGO WHEN ELIZABETH JANEWAY RAISED A GLASS TO ME AND SAID, "HERE'S TO THE NEXT TEN YEARS!" I, FOR THE FIRST TIME, UNDERSTOOD THAT THE FEMINIST PRESS WAS MORE THAN THE "MOVE-MENT" ORGANIZATION I HAD HELPED TO FOUND IN 1970. IN 1970, MY VISION WAS LIMITED: HOW COULD IT HAVE BEEN OTHERWISE? I WAS REARED TO BELIEVE THAT THE WORLD WAS A RATIONAL PLACE, THAT "CULTURE" WAS ARRANGED IN PRESCRIBED MODULES OFFERED AS COLLEGE COURSES, AND THAT INTELLIGENT, EVEN LEARNED WOMEN MIGHT OCCUPY AN AMBIVALENT SPACE IN A WORLD CLEARLY DEFINED AS BELONGING TO MEN. THE BEST WRITERS, I WAS TAUGHT, AND I TAUGHT IN RETURN, WERE MEN.

In 1970, when I read Tillie Olsen's tattered photocopy of *Life in the Iron Mills,* published anonymously (at Rebecca Harding Davis's request) in the *Atlantic* in 1861, that vision shattered. If this powerful novella had been "lost," this author "silenced," then perhaps what I knew as "culture" was but half of the story. Of course, hundreds of other women scholars (and a few men) were making similar discoveries at about that time, not only in literature, but in history, anthropology, psychology, and other disciplines. A new area of knowledge, women's studies, was being carved out of these discoveries. And with *Life in the Iron Mills* published as its first "reprint" in 1972, The Feminist Press began the work of restoring to its rightful place in the cultural life of the United States the literature of women writers. In 1973, we published *Daughter of Earth* by Agnes Smedley and *The Yellow Wallpaper* by Charlotte Perkins Gilman, and began the search for rights to Zora Neale Hurston's work, published in 1979 as an an-

thology edited by Alice Walker, *I Love Myself When I Am Laughing...And Then Again When I Am Looking Mean and Impressive.*

By 1980, we had published some fifty books; and yet, I could still assume that our work would be taken over by "regular" presses, that we were but a "temporary" organization, useful chiefly to stimulate that process. Indeed, that process took hold in the 1980s, when trade, university, and other small presses—including new feminist presses—began to announce series that "discovered" women writers of the past, often reprinting work we had declined in the 1970s as not being "perfect" enough.

Remember that, even in the early 1980s, African-American women writers were not high on anyone's list except ours: We published Paule Marshall's *Brown Girl, Brownstones* in 1981; *The Living Is Easy* by Dorothy West and *But Some of Us Are Brave: Black Women's Studies* in 1982; *Reena and Other Stories* by Paule Marshall in 1983; and *Daddy Was a Number Runner* by Louise Meriwether and *This Child's Gonna Live* by Sarah E. Wright in 1986. By 1986, African-American writers were being courted for their work, and we were honored to have been chosen by Meriwether and Wright.

Nineteen eighty was a pivotal year for The Feminist Press in another significant way: Mariam Chamberlain, then a program officer at the Ford Foundation, insisted that the time was right for U.S. women's studies pioneers to turn their attention to Europe and beyond. With her support, and that of the Ford Foundation, The Feminist Press became the coordinator of Women's Studies International, responsible for programs at United Nations-sponsored conferences in Copenhagen in 1980, in Nairobi in 1985, and now in Beijing in 1995. Quite naturally, such work led to questions about women writers in countries outside the United States. In Europe, feminist presses were already at work, but not elsewhere.

In the 1980s, The Feminist Press began to search for an Indian editor who would attempt to find "lost" women writers of India, a project that eventually took almost a decade to complete. We have now begun to consider even more ambitious projects in Africa, Latin America, and Eastern Europe. Everywhere, we have met similar responses from the publishing establishment and academe: "There were no women writers," we are told. Or, "If there were any, they weren't any good. Else they'd be in print." Major publishers in India and Britain were uninterested in *Women Writing in India: 600 B.C. to the Present* (in two volumes) until after they had seen the published books. Then the skepticism disappeared, and, at least in India, there is currently a renaissance in the reissuing of "lost" women writers, not only in English, but in their original major Indian languages.

From the first, we assumed a nonideological stance about feminism. Our definition was typically generic: *Feminism means the action by women and men to establish equality and justice for women. It is, in fact, the only fe-*

male-gendered word in English that includes both women and men. We were going to contribute to that goal by publishing literature by women that was also of historical value, for we agreed that one could not act in the present for the future without a knowledge of the past. Hence, history is an essential ingredient of feminism.

I remember teaching *Life in the Iron Mills* in the summer of 1978 to German graduate students baffled by its inclusion not only in my course, but in The Feminist Press's catalog. "What makes this work feminist?" they wanted to know. I was hard put to explain, since they understood feminism quite narrowly as the ideology of change in the present. Rebecca Harding Davis focuses not on gender at all, but on class, and if one understands that in the border city of Wheeling, West Virginia, Welsh immigrants were lumped with African Americans, it's also about race. The men are treated no better than the women: Life is impoverished, brutal, and brief. We published it because it is an exquisitely strong rendering of lives silenced not only by poverty, but by what Muriel Rukeyser calls "despisals." We published it because we could assume also that the middle-class Quaker woman's sympathy for the silenced may have been aroused by her own gendered silencing. After the novella had been declared a work of "genius" by Nathaniel Hawthorne, and the sex of the writer revealed, she could, nevertheless, not accept an invitation to be feted in Boston until her brother returned from the Civil War to act as her escort.

Today, many years after that encounter with German students, would I say anything different about the importance of Rebecca Harding Davis's work? Probably I would add one new urgent element: the danger of modern amnesia. For the work of rediscovery is not finished; and those rediscovered must not be allowed to disappear once again. Perhaps I am unnecessarily gloomy. On many days I see the cup of achievement half full, rather than half empty. But I worry: I worry about the privileged young women who believe that since they can do anything they want to do, there's no need for feminism; I worry about the bookstore buyers who regard *Life in the Iron Mills* as "dated" rather than as valuable as Dickens's *Hard Times* (in my opinion, a lesser work); I worry about the male (and a few female) professors who still teach only male writers or only male history; I worry about a new generation of female scholars, not many of whom have been taught by feminist pioneers of my generation, but by scholars mouthing a new jargon that silences gender, race, and class. I worry.

And yet, one can point with pride to the 125 feminist bookstores in the U.S. that exist because it is now possible to fill hundreds of shelves with thousands of books and periodicals by and about women, ninety-nine percent of which were published or republished only during the past twenty-five years. One can also point to the growth of women's studies programs over the same period: 620 programs and courses—too many to count—on every campus in the country, as well as eighty centers for research on women. And abroad, on every continent, similar patterns either well developed or just begun in the early years of the 1990s. Not surprisingly, one can also see vast changes in the lives especially of privileged women: They are now more free to work in paid employment, to run for political office, to borrow money either for housing or business ventures, to choose work in nontraditional professions or trades.

On the other hand, the majority of nonliterates around the world are women; in developing countries, the poorest of the poor are women, a growing number of whom head households. In Europe and the U.S. as well as in developing countries, women hold a minority of academic positions, a smaller minority of positions in politics and on governing boards in business and elsewhere. Women are often still unrecognized or "lost" as artists and writers.

All of which means that for The Feminist Press and other feminist institutions, the work has only begun. The first twenty-five years may have been the easiest, in fact, for it is often more difficult to maintain an organization than to found it in the first place. Publishing is still a "business," and the *business* of social change requires not only a different perspective but different strategies. Hard work may lie ahead, but now I can be the first to say, "Here's to the next twenty-five years!"

FLORENCE HOWE is director and publisher of The Feminist Press at CUNY and professor of English at the City College and the Graduate Center, CUNY. A former president of the Modern Language Association, she is author of *Myths of Coeducation: Selected Essays, 1964-1983* and editor of *No More Masks! An Anthology of American Women Poets.*

Photo by Mary Warshaw.

Happy Birthday to Us and Many More to Come

Helene D. Goldfarb

WHEN THE FEMINIST PRESS BEGAN IN 1970, FEW WOULD HAVE EXPECTED THIS DARING AND QUIXOTIC GRASSROOTS EXPERIMENT IN EDUCATION AND LITERATURE WOULD GROW INTO THE WORLD-RESPECTED ACADEMIC INSTITUTION THAT IT IS TODAY.

How did I become involved in the work of The Press? Florence Howe and I go back to our days as Hunter College undergraduates, when she and I were interested in making things happen through student government (we were both presidents of the Student Self-Government Association) and were founding members of the only non-sectarian, interracial sorority on campus. I was finishing my junior year when she graduated in 1950 but we kept in touch.

Over the years, our paths took different turns—she left New York and I stayed. Our meeting when she returned to New York in 1971 was most inauspicious—we bumped into each other at Lord and Taylor's in Manhasset. She introduced me to The Press, which had recently relocated on the campus of the State University of New York, College at Old Westbury. To say that I became interested would be an understatement. I was intrigued and I gladly accepted an invitation to join the Board of Directors.

As The Press has grown over the years so has the work of the Board. We are still looking for "lost" women writers to publish, but we have also introduced children's literature to our agenda, as well as Asian, European, African, Latin American, and Australian writers, often finding treasures in unexpected places. We have also begun publishing a memoir series, a travel series, and a feminist cookbook.

All of this takes money and dedication. And so, it has increasingly become the responsibility of the Board of Directors to raise funds to keep projects going and growing. We are responsible for the budget and all other financial decisions. It is our responsibility to oversee the workings of The Press as well as the work of The Press.

The members of the Board of Directors have always been a diverse group of women and men from a variety of backgrounds. Members serve on committees, raise funds, attend meetings and other events. They give more than their time and their money; they give their expertise and commitment. I speak for all of us when I say that working as a Board member is a rewarding experience. We look forward to continued gratifying service.

HELENE D. GOLDFARB is key counselor at the Albert Leonard Middle School in New Rochelle. She has been president of the Hunter College Alumni Association and serves on its board as well as on the board of the Lenox Hill Neighborhood House.

PUBLICATIONS AND POLICIES COMMITTEE

Meena Alexander

Tuzyline Jita Allan

Electa Arenal

Nina Auerbach

Margot Badran

Shari Benstock

Bella Brodski

Abena P.A. Busia

Moira Ferguson

Liza Fiol-Matta

Jane Gottlieb

Maryemma Graham

Barbara Hampton

Sorrel Hays

Elaine Hedges

Dorothy Helly

Nancy Rose Hunt

Rounaq Jahan

Elizabeth Janeway

Ketu Katrak

Roberta Lamb

Nellie Y. McKay

Jane Marcus

Judith Miller

Valerie Miner

Andree Nicola-McLaughlin

Tillie Olsen

Daphne Patai

Linda Perkins

Barbara Sicherman

Kathryn Kish Sklar

Susan Squier

Judith Stitzel

Amy Swerdlow

Elizabeth Wood

STAFF AND CONSULTANTS

Tuzyline Jita Allan

Consultant, Women Writing in Africa Project

Abena P.A. Busia

Consultant, Women Writing in Africa Project

Sara Clough

Editorial Assistant and Assistant to the Publisher

Alyssa Colton

Assistant Editor

Susan Cozzi

Associate Director and Marketing Director

Franklin Dennis

Consultant, Publicity

Susannah Driver

Senior Editor and Foreign Rights Manager

Jim Frederick

Assistant to the Publisher

Florence Howe

Director and Publisher

Tina R. Malaney

Design and Production Manager

Dianne Schwartz

Consultant, Beijing Project

Sarah Stovin

Customer Service Associate

Rachel Weiss

Marketing and Publicity Assistant

THE FEMINIST PRESS'S
FIRST TWENTY-FIVE YEARS

1970

—The Feminist Press is founded in Baltimore, Maryland by Florence Howe and Paul Lauter. The first office is located at their home and the first meeting is held on November 17.

1971

—The Press moves to the State University of New York, College at Old Westbury, where Florence Howe has been appointed professor of humanities.

—The Press publishes its first book, Barbara Danish's *The Dragon and the Doctor*, the story of a girl doctor and her younger brother, a nurse.

1972

—*Women's Studies Newsletter* begins publication, and the Clearinghouse on Women's Studies moves from the Modern Language Association, both to become educational projects at The Feminist Press.

—The Press receives its first grants from the D.J.B. Foundation and the Coordinating Council of Literary Magazines, both for general support. The Rockefeller Family Fund awards The Press a grant for a series of community workshops on sexism in children's books, held in Old Westbury, Long Island; Baltimore, Maryland; and South Hadley, Massachusetts.

—The Press publishes three pamphlets and five books, including its first volume of rediscovered feminist literary classics, *Life in the Iron Mills*, a novella by Rebecca Harding Davis originally published by the *Atlantic* in 1861. This edition includes a biographical interpretation by Tillie Olsen.

1973

—The Press establishes a reprints advisory committee.

—The Press begins college internships in publishing.

—The Press offers its first in-service course in women's studies—"Sex-Role Stereotyping in the Schools"—to thirty-five teachers from Long Island and other New York area elementary and secondary school instructors. Two additional courses are offered in the Manhasset and Glen Cove school districts.

—The Press receives grants from the Cummins Engine Foundation, the Ford Foundation, the Rockefeller Family Fund, and a subcontract from the Resource Center on Sex-Roles Education of the National Education Association, all for special projects.

—The Press publishes three pamphlets and eight books, including *The Yellow Wallpaper* by Charlotte Perkins Gilman, with an afterword by Elaine Hedges.

1974

—With a grant from the Rockefeller Family Fund, The Press hosts an innovative conference, "Re-educating a Generation of Teachers," which brings together teachers and administrators from twelve cities to plan education programs in women's studies.

—The Press publishes two pamphlets and six books, including the ground-breaking *Who's Who and Where in Women's Studies*, funded by the Ford Foundation and edited by Tamar Berkowitz, Jean Mangi, and Jane Williamson.

1975

—The Press moves into its new home, a little brown house in the woods on the campus of SUNY, College at Old Westbury, with the help of a grant from the Research Foundation/SUNY.

—The Press receives a subcontract from the Schlesinger Library, Radcliffe College, for the preparation of *The Maimie Papers*, a project funded by the National Endowment for the Humanities.

—The Press receives two major grants from the Ford Foundation and the Carnegie Corporation to begin the seven-year Women's Lives/Women's Work project aimed at developing, field-testing, and publishing twelve books with accompanying teaching guides for the senior high school and college classroom.

—The Press publishes two pamphlets and four books.

1976

—Elizabeth Janeway hosts a fund-raising party for The Press on April 19, where she speaks about women and literature. Tillie Olsen, Grace Paley, and Adrienne Rich read from their work.

—*Women's Studies Newsletter* is declared a national resource for the fledgling National Women's Studies Association.

—In-service courses continue; other courses in publishing begin; the staff organizes three book parties and many speaking engagements.

—The Press publishes six books, including *Käthe Kollwitz: Woman and Artist*, a biography by Martha Kearns, and Agnes Smedley's *Portraits of Chinese Women in Revolution*, edited by Jan MacKinnon and Steve MacKinnon.

1977

—*Women's Studies Newsletter* becomes the official journal of the National Women's Studies Association. This relationship ends in 1982.

—Florence Howe, on a Fulbright Award, attends the First International Women and Development Conference in India in November.

—The Press publishes three books, including *The Maimie Papers*, edited by Ruth Rosen and Sue Davidson.

1978

—The Press teaches its seventeenth in-service course.

—The Press is awarded additional funding for Women's Lives/ Women's Work by the Ford Foundation, the Carnegie Corporation, the Rockefeller Family Fund, and new funding by the Hazen Foundation. Field-testing of the books continues.

—The Press publishes three books, including the best-selling children's book *Tatterhood and Other Tales*, by Ethel Johnston Phelps.

1979

—The Press's staff, which has acted as its own board of directors for nine years, appoints an external board of directors, to begin functioning in 1980.

—The Press receives additional funding for Women's Lives/ Women's Work from the National Endowment for the Humanities.

—The Press publishes three pamphlets and nine books, including a Zora Neale Hurston reader entitled *I Love Myself When I Am Laughing…And Then Again When I Am Looking Mean and Impressive*, edited by Alice Walker, signalling a commitment to African-American women writers a decade ahead of the major publishing houses. Four of the other books published are the first in the Women's Lives/Women's Work series: *Women Working: An Anthology of Stories and Poems; Black Foremothers: Three Lives; Out of the Bleachers: Writings on Women and Sport;* and *Rights and Wrongs: Women's Struggle for Legal Equality.*

1980

—The Press celebrates its tenth birthday with dramatic readings by Geraldine Fitzgerald, Mary Alice, Jean Marsh, Colleen Dewhurst, Ruby Dee, Viveca Lindfors, and Vinie Burrows, directed by Midge Mackenzie.

—With funding from the Ford Foundation, The Press coordinates two weeks of panels and round tables on women's studies at the United Nations NGO Forum held in Copenhagen. At this conference, Florence Howe and Vina Mazumdar of the Center for Women's Development Studies in New Delhi, India, form Women's Studies International, a global network of women's resource and research centers.

—The Press receives grants from the Ms. Foundation, the Rockefeller Family Fund, the Women's Educational Equity Act Program, and the Fund for the Improvement of Post-Secondary Education (FIPSE). The FIPSE grant funds the development and publication of *Everywoman's Guide to Colleges and Universities.*

—The Press publishes two pamphlets and five books

1981

—*Women's Studies Newsletter*, expanded and redesigned, becomes the *Women's Studies Quarterly.*

—The Press receives grants from the New York Community Trust to work in eight New York City schools in a reading intervention program, from the Ford Foundation for *Women's Studies International*, and from the Fund for the Improvement of Post-Secondary Education for *Reconstructing American Literature.*

—The Press publishes ten pamphlets and six books, five of which complete the Women's Lives/Women's Work series, and the sixth of which is Paule Marshall's *Brown Girl, Brownstones.*

1982

—The Press suffers a serious fire on September 19. Production is halted then slowly resumed, and most of the building remains boarded up for seven months. The staff continues to work on four major projects.

—The Press publishes one pamphlet and seven books, including the entirely new *Everywoman's Guide to Colleges and Universities*, and the two ground-breaking curriculum guides that become best-sellers: *Lesbian Studies: Past and Present* and *All the Women Are White, All the Blacks Are Men, But Some of Us Are Brave: Black Women's Studies.*

1983

—SUNY begins repairs on the building in April.

—The Press receives a grant from the Women's Education Equity Act Program for an anthology of literature by and about disabled women; a grant from the Ford Foundation for Women's Studies International; and small grants for general support of the publishing program from the New York State Council for the Arts, AT&T, Mobil Oil, and the United Church Board for Homeland Ministries.

—The Press publishes seven books.

1984

—The Press signs a distribution agreement with Harper and Row.

—The Press signs several agreements with Indiana University Press and begins discussion about moving to Indiana University.

—The Press agrees to give its archives to the Schlesinger Library, Radcliffe College.

—The Press receives grants from the Rockefeller Foundation, the Women's Educational Equity Act Program, the New York State Council on the Arts, and several smaller awards.

—The Press publishes five books, including a volume compiled by Tillie Olsen in honor of the The Press's forthcoming fifteenth anniversary, called *Mother to Daughter, Daughter to Mother: A Feminist Press Daybook and Reader.*

1985

—In January, at a special meeting of the Board of Directors, The Feminist Press accepts an invitation from Chancellor Joseph S. Murphy to move into residence at The City University of New York (CUNY). On September ll, at a ceremony hosted by the chancellor and the board of trustees of CUNY, the agreement between The Feminist Press and CUNY is signed.

—The Press celebrates both its fifteenth anniversary and its recent move with a party hosted by Donna Shalala, then president of Hunter College, where Toni Morrison reads from her then unpublished novel *Beloved.* Other anniversary parties are held in Louisville, Kentucky; Portland, Oregon; Newton Center, Massachusetts; and in Manhattan, where Grace Paley and Tillie Olsen give readings.

—The Press receives several grants in support of its move into residence at CUNY.

—With support from the Ford-funded Women's Studies International project, The Press organizes panels and round tables at the United Nations NGO Forum in Nairobi.

—The Press publishes nine books, including a new, expanded edition of *Life in the Iron Mills.*

1986

—*A Day at a Time: The Diary Literature of American Women from 1764 to the Present* receives the prestigious Pushcart Prize. The Quality Book Club issues an edition of *A Day at a Time.*

—The Press receives grants from the AT&T Foundation and the L.J. Skaggs and Mary C. Skaggs Foundation.

—The Press publishes twelve books, including all four bilingual volumes of the Defiant Muse: Feminist Poems from the Middle Ages to the Present series. Spanish, German, Italian and French editions are published.

1987

—The Press receives grants from the Ford Foundation, the Skaggs Foundation, and the New York State Council on the Arts.

—The Press publishes one pamphlet and nine books, including *With Wings*, its first anthology of literary work by women with disabilities, edited by Marsha Saxton and Florence Howe; and a new edition of *Daughter of Earth* by Agnes Smedley, with a foreword by Alice Walker and an afterword by Nancy Hoffman.

1988

—The Talman Company becomes The Press's new distributor.

—The Press resumes its childen's book publishing program, focusing on ages ten and older.

—The Press celebrates its eighteenth anniversary with a party at the New York Public Library. Awards are given to Elaine Hedges, Elizabeth Janeway, Toni Morrison, Tillie Olsen, and Alice Walker.

—The Press receives grants from the Population Council and from the New York State Council on the Arts.

—The Press publishes nine books, including *Sultana's Dream*, its first volume from the Indian subcontinent.

1989

—The Press holds a party upon the publication of *How I Wrote Jubilee and Other Essays on Life and Literature* by Margaret Walker, who receives a Feminist Press award.

—*Islanders* earns *Art Direction* magazine's Certificate of Distinction for Creativity, Best Book Jacket Design.

—The Press receives grants from the Ford Foundation, the Ms. Magazine Educational Foundation, the National Endowment for the Arts, the New York State Council on the Arts, the Sophia Fund, and the AAUW Foundation.

—The Press publishes twelve books, including the unique *Lone Voyagers: Academic Women in Coeducational Universities, 1870-1937*, edited by Geraldine Jonçich Clifford.

1990

—*What Did Miss Darrington See?* edited by Jessica Amanda Salmonson, wins the Lambda Literary Award for lesbian science fiction and the Readercon Small Press Award for Best Anthology.

—Diane Peacock Jezic, author of *Women Composers*, is posthumously awarded the 1989 Pauline Alderman Prize for New Scholarship on Women in Music from the International Congress on Women in Music.

—The Press wins the coveted Carey Thomas Award from *Publishers Weekly* for twenty years of creative publishing.

—The Press receives grants from the Global Fund for Women, the New York State Council on the Arts, and the Foundation for a Compassionate Society.

—The Press publishes eight books, including the National Gallery's *Eva/Ave: Woman in Renaissance and Baroque Prints.*

1991

—The Press is the only recipient of all three grants awarded competitively by the Council of Literary Magazines and Presses, funded by the Lila Wallace—Reader's Digest Literary Publishers Marketing Development Program. The Press is one of five publishers awarded a major two-year grant for developing a marketing program.

—The Press announces the Diane Peacock Jezic Women and Music series.

—The Press receives grants from the National Endowment for the Arts, the National Endowment for the Humanities, and the New York State Council on the Arts.

—The Press publishes eight books, including the first volume of *Women Writing in India: 600 B.C. to the Present,* edited by Susie Tharu and K. Lalita.

1992

—In February and March, The Press holds fund-raising events—with readings from its books by actresses—at B. Smith's Restaurant in Manhattan.

—*Women Writing in India: 600 B.C. to the Early Twentieth Century* receives the Best Book of the Year Award from the *Book Review* (India). Indian rights are sold to Oxford University Press.

—The Press receives grants from the National Endowment for the Arts, the National Endowment for the Humanities, the New York State Council on the Arts, the Fund for a Compassionate Society, and the Dougherty Foundation. In addition, at the very end of the year, The Press receives a challenge grant of $250,000 from the Ford Foundation.

—The Press publishes seven books, including the first three volumes in its new Cross-Cultural Memoir series: *I Dwell in Possibility, Lion Woman's Legacy,* and *The Seasons.*

1993

—Consortium Book Sales and Distribution in St. Paul, Minnesota, becomes The Press's new distributor.

—The Board of Directors authorizes a new series of travel books as well as a feminist cookbook.

—The Press gives an eightieth birthday party for Elizabeth Janeway at the home of Board member Sue Rosenberg Zalk.

—The Press receives grants from the Luchek Family Charitable Trust the Sister Fund, the New York State Council on the Arts, and the Population Council.

—The Press receives a grant from the Ford Foundation to fund a series of national reports on women's studies to be given at the Fifth International Interdisciplinary Conference on Women, held in Costa Rica in February.

—The Press publishes six books, including the novel *Changes,* by African author Ama Ata Aidoo, and the second volume of *Women Writing in India: 600 B.C. to the Present,* which again wins the Best Book of the Year Award from the *Book Review* (India).

1994

—On a grant from the Ford Foundation, The Press holds a meeting in Accra, Ghana, to initiate planning for a new project called Women Writing in Africa.

—The Board of Directors institutes a retirement plan for the staff through TIAA/CREF.

—Gazelle Book Services Limited in Lancaster, England, becomes The Press's European distributor.

—The Press receives grants from the New York State Council on the Arts, the Paul Rapaport Foundation, the Rabinowitz Foundation, the Catherine and John T. MacArthur Foundation, the Ms. Magazine Education Foundation, Keystone Laboratories, and the Menke Foundation. A grant from the Ford Foundation will fund national reports on women's studies at sessions in Beijing, as well as an educational resource center.

—With a grant from the AT&T Foundation, The Press begins work on *Re-Visioning Feminism Around the World.*

—The Press publishes nine books, including its first travel book, *Australia for Women,* launched simultaneously at the Feminist Book Fair in Australia by The Feminist Press, Spinifex Press (Australia), and Frauenoffensive (Germany).

THE
FEMMY AWARDS

THE FEMMY AWARDS ARE PRESENTED TO WOMEN AND MEN WHO HAVE MADE A SIGNIFICANT CONTRIBUTION TO THE WORK OF THE FEMINIST PRESS, AND HENCE TO EQUALITY AND JUSTICE FOR WOMEN. BEGINNING IN 1985, WE GAVE AWARDS TO THE FOLLOWING PEOPLE, HENCE-FORTH FEMMY AWARDEES ALL:

ELAINE HEDGES
ELIZABETH JANEWAY
PAULE MARSHALL
TILLIE OLSEN
TONI MORRISON
NIDA E. THOMAS
GENEVIEVE VAUGHAN
ALICE WALKER
MARGARET WALKER

IN 1995
FEMMY AWARDEES ARE:

Mariam K. Chamberlain

MARIAM K. CHAMBERLAIN
Founding President of the
National Council for Research on Women
Former Program Officer at the Ford Foundation
Board member and author of The Feminist Press

Johnnetta B. Cole

JOHNNETTA B. COLE
President of Spelman College
Honorary Board member and author of The Feminist Press
Photo by Bud Smith photo.

JOSEPH CUNNINGHAM
CEO and President of Creative Graphics Inc., Allentown, Pennsylvannia
Typesetter and Benefactor of The Feminist Press

Helene D. Goldfarb

HELENE D. GOLDFARB
Key Counselor at the Albert Leonard Middle School, New Rochelle, New York
Chair of the Board of The Feminist Press

Joseph Cunningham

DOROTHY HART
Vice President for Finance of McNaughton & Gunn Inc., Saline, Michigan
Printer and Benefactor of The Feminist Press

Grace Paley

GRACE PALEY
Prizewinning author and fundraiser for The Feminist Press
Photo by Gentyl and Hyers/Arts Council.

Dorothy Hart

PAUL POMBO
Partner in Moses & Schreiber, LLP, Lake Success, New York
Accountant for The Feminist Press

Paul Pombo

NANCY PORTER
Professor of English and Director of Graduate Study, Portland State University
Editor of the Women's Studies Quarterly, 1982-1992

Nancy Porter

DONNA E. SHALALA
Secretary of Health and Human Services, Washington, D.C.
Former President of Hunter College, The City University of New York
Friend of The Feminist Press

Donna E. Shalala

New World Aria

Meena Alexander

I SEE A CITY FILLED WITH WOMEN. NO, I MUST CORRECT THAT. THE WOMEN ARE NOT VISIBLE YET. I SEE SMALL FIRES, IN GARBAGE CANS, BY THE PARK BENCHES, TWIGS SMOLDERING AT THE EDGE OF DOORWAYS SHIELDED BY DARKNESS. THE FIRES BRISTLE, THEN SLOWLY WITH A GREAT ROARING, RISE INTO THE AIR. THE TREES BY THE RIVER GLOW IN THE HEAT AND BIRDS HIDDEN IN THE LEAVES START TO SING. DRIVEN OUT BY THE HEAT, AS IF THEY THEMSELVES HAD NOT SET THE FLAMES ROARING WITH CANS OF KEROSENE, WITH TINY MATCH BOXES PILFERED FROM KITCHEN AND RESTAURANT, THE WOMEN COME RUNNING. HUNDREDS, THOUSANDS OF THEM, A MOUNTAIN OF WOMEN GATHERED BY THE RIVER. RIVER WATER TURNS ROSY WITH FIERY REFLECTIONS FROM THE FLAMES FALLING OFF THE TALL GLASS BUILDINGS IN THE DOWNTOWN PART OF THE CITY. SUDDENLY I HEAR A SHARP VOICE CRYING, "WHERE ARE THE CHILDREN?" THEN LOUDER, "WHERE ARE THE MEN?" THE MOUNTAIN STARTS TO QUIVER. SOMEONE LIFTS UP HER GREY SKIRTS, ANOTHER HER TORN BLACK SARI. ARMS AND LEGS POKE OUT, BEARDS, THIGHS, HAIRY CHESTS, TINY QUIVERING LIPS. IN ALL THAT CACOPHONY, AS MEN AND CHILDREN STUMBLE OUT TO SAFETY, I LISTEN TO A SHORT WOMAN SINGING. SHE CANNOT SING VERY WELL BUT HER VOICE HELPS. IN THAT AWKWARD MUSIC SOMEONE PASSES OUT BITS OF BREAD—NO MATTER THAT IT IS HARD AND MOLDY. ANOTHER POURS OUT MILK. WHERE DID SHE FIND THAT OLD PITCHER, MILK BLUE AT THE RIM? A THIRD STARTS SLICING APPLES, THE FRUIT RESTING ON A STONE. A FOURTH, LEAN AND HUNGRY, HER HAIR TIED BACK WITH A DARK SCARF STARES BACK, "YES, YES," SHE WHISPERS, "THE OLD CITY MUST BURN." I THINK SHE MUTTERS SOMETHING ABOUT LEARNING HOW TO BUILD, BUT HIDDEN IN THE OVERHANGING TREE, BODY DRENCHED WITH SWEAT, I LOSE HER WORDS. I SHALL FALL, I THINK, BREAK ARMS, LEGS, SPLIT MY LIPS INTO TINY MORSELS. I SHALL BE SILENCED ENTIRELY, OR SPEAK IN ODD, UNINTELLIGIBLE TONGUES. MY MOTHER'S EYES—SHE LEFT ME SO VERY MANY YEARS AGO AND I WAS FORCED TO FEND FOR MYSELF BY THE RIVER BANK, PICKING UP SCRAPS OF FOOD, USING LEAVES TO WIPE MY BLOOD, SLEEPING IN TREES— FLASH BEFORE ME. JUST AS I SENSE I AM FALLING INTO THAT FIERY DARKNESS I CATCH THE VOICES OF TEN THOUSAND WOMEN, NO LONGER STRANGERS TO EACH OTHER, SINGING.

MEENA ALEXANDER, a poet and novelist, is author of the memoir *Fault Lines* **(The Feminist Press, 1993). She is professor of English at Hunter College and the Graduate Center, CUNY.**

Photo by Colleen McKay.

Mothering the Father in Me

Tuzyline Jita Allan

IN A SOCIETY THAT WAS (AND STILL IS) UNAPOLOGETICALLY MASCULINE, MY FORMATIVE INFLUENCES CAME FROM A MAN WHO EXUDED CHARM, GENEROSITY, AND A SPIRITUAL LARGESSE, QUALITIES THAT WERE WOVEN INTO THE FABRIC OF FEMALE LIFE IN MY HOMETOWN OF SHENGE, A COASTAL HAMLET FACING THE MASSIVE ATLANTIC OCEAN IN SIERRA LEONE, WEST AFRICA. TEACHER, PASTOR, VETERAN FARMER, AND FISHERMAN, MY FATHER MADE NO SECRET OF HIS HERITABLE TIES TO AFRICAN CULTURE AND ITS PREDILECTION FOR THE MALE GENDER. THAT IS, UNTIL I WAS BORN, AS I LATER LEARNED FROM MY MOTHER. HAVING A GIRL, NOT THE EXPECTED BOY, AS HIS FIRST-BORN, MY FATHER NEGOTIATED HIS DISAPPOINTMENT BY SIMULTANEOUSLY RAISING EXPECTATIONS ABOUT MY WORTHINESS AS HIS HEIR AND LOWERING THE CULTURAL PITCH FOR MALE SUPREMACY. WITH THE FORMER ACT, HE ANTICIPATED NO DEFEAT: HE SUPERVISED MY READING AND WRITING AT HOME LONG BEFORE I STARTED SCHOOL TO ENSURE A SWIFT AND SUCCESSFUL CLIMB UP THE EDUCATIONAL LADDER. THE

No Suppressing

Electa Arenal

VITALITY TRANSLATED INTO ACTION. OLD BOOKS REPRINTED. NEW ONES MADE. ONCE KNOWN AS THE PRESS OF SAD ENDINGS. FEMINISM: FLUID, FLAMBOY-ANT, FLEXIBLE, FRAMING OF NEW IDEAS, FANTASTICALLY RESOURCEFUL.

How has my feminism changed in the last twenty-five years? Let me encapsulate the ways it hasn't. The love affair certainly isn't over because it is with a world-view that re-sees, re-knows, re-visions, re-edits, that makes room, gives space, reproves and improves this place (planet) we call home.

Twenty-five years ago I was teaching at the no-longer-extant Richmond College, a new branch of CUNY where one of the first women's studies programs was organized, and where I was given the opportunity to devise—to the taunt of "What women writers?!"—one of the first courses in the country on women writers of Spain and Latin America.

What is important to the future of feminism? A continuing critique (of the "malestream" and of itself); inclusivity; specificity; keeping the academy open; watering the grass roots.

Excerpt from a journal entry, August 29th, 1994: A cool breeze comes through the window. Traffic begins to rumble over the asphalt, heavily. I still hear New York din over a scrim of Bergen, Norway's silence. I'm ill at ease. On overload. Toes need tending. Legs too. Too rushed after first evening class. Too tired after too little sleep. Grammar. Gertrude Stein. The ligaments of talk. Her experiments have fascinated me for years. Incomprehensible? Prehensible. Playing, pointing at what we ignore, highlighting color, tone, structure   At times we do this at times we do that   We do that   I do   Do you?   At times I do

In her spirit: To the Feminist Press   The Press   The Feminist Press   Twenty-five years at press impressing, in press The Feminist Press   Feminist   Press   No suppressing the Feminist Press How express the pressing need for such a press?

ELECTA ARENAL is professor of Spanish at the College of Staten Island and the Graduate Center, CUNY. She is coeditor and cotranslator with Amanda Powell of *The Answer/La Respuesta* by Sor Juana Inés de la Cruz (The Feminist Press, 1994).

Photo by Joseph Singer.

LATTER, HOWEVER, IN THIS MALE PRESERVE, WAS A HARDER SELL, AND SO, RATHER THAN RECOMMENDING A REMEDY, HE DECIDED TO LIVE IT. MY FATHER BROKE LONG-STANDING TRADITION BY DOING WOMEN'S WORK, SUCH AS WASHING AND IRONING HIS CLOTHES, SWEEPING THE YARD, AND COOKING THE FAMILY MEAL ONCE A WEEK. OUTSIDE OUR HOME, HE STRETCHED HIS SENSE OF CIVIC DUTY TO INCLUDE A RISKY BUT PRINCIPLED STAND AGAINST WIFE BEATING, THE DEVALUATION OF GIRL CHILDREN, AND THE ECONOMIC INEQUITIES OF WIDOWS AND DIVORCED WOMEN.

This subversive dynamic provides a glimpse of how I managed to step out of a gendered destiny into the wider reaches of humanity. I am today what my mother could not become, in spite of her boundless intelligence and creative energy, because she had no access to an emotional lifeline. The feminist revolution of the 1960s threw many women this lifeline and with it, the promise that they will not be stampeded by gender difference. It is the vision that prompted my father's brave leap into a cultural breach many years ago, one that I will work hard to mother—for my daughter's sake.

TUZYLINE JITA ALLAN is associate professor of English at Baruch College, CUNY. She is author of *Literature Around the Globe, Aesthetics: A Comparative Review*, and *Womanist and Feminist Aesthetics*, which won the 1993 Northeast Modern Languages Book Award. She contributed the afterword to *Changes*, a novel by Ama Ata Aidoo (The Feminist Press, 1994).

Athletes, Engineers, Computer Jocks

—The Future We Never Envisioned: Women's Studies and General Education Requirements

Arlene Voski Avakian

IT IS JANUARY 1994, THE MIDDLE OF ONE OF THE WORST WINTERS IN RECENT MEMORY. ON MY WAY TO THE FIRST CLASS OF WOMEN'S STUDIES 187, "INTRODUCTION TO WOMEN'S STUDIES," I CARRY THE BOX CONTAINING THE MORE THAN THREE HUNDRED COPIES OF THE EIGHT-PAGE SYLLABUS FOR THE COURSE. I WALK WITH FIVE TEACHING ASSISTANTS TO THE LARGE AUDITORIUM WHERE MANY OF THE SEATS ARE ALREADY FILLED WITH STUDENTS WHO HAVE COME EARLY TO ENSURE THEIR ENROLLMENT IN CLASS. MANY MORE STUDENTS SIGN UP FOR THIS COURSE THAN WE CAN ADMIT. THREE HUNDRED IS THE LIMIT OF THE ROOM AND THE EDGE OF MY TOLERANCE.

It didn't begin this way. Twenty years ago the curriculum of the two-year pilot program in women's studies at the University of Massachusetts/Amherst was based on the idea that classes in women's studies were places where feminist faculty and feminist students met in small groups to share their lives as women. Courses explored what had been until then banished—women's lives, women's experiences, our experiences. Together we were to find ways to change the world. Developed by a committee of faculty, staff, and undergraduate and graduate students working collaboratively, the proposal for this experiment proclaimed women's studies to be an academic program based on scholarship by and about women, most of it new, but some of it newly discovered in the late 1960s and early 1970s by this second wave of feminists, and all of it ground-breaking. That was the face we showed to the Faculty Senate, which approved the proposal in the spring of 1974, but the dream that many of us had for this new program was that it would create a new academy, one built on feminist principles.

It is almost time for the class to begin. I look out at the women and men streaming into the room, and I think about those beginnings as I always do when I teach this class. I raise the microphone to my lips and speak into it, signaling that I will always begin promptly at 10:10 whether students are in their seats or not. I welcome them to the class, stating both the class number and name to be sure that everyone is where they think they are, and I ask those in the last row if they can hear. One or two heads nod, while others are still talking or already have the glazed look of students in large classes.

Now that I have formally begun the class, some students take out their notebooks and the teaching assistants begin distributing the syllabus, a document developed over the more than ten years I have been teaching this course. That, at least, has been a collective effort. My colleague, Sandi Morgen, and I developed it together years ago and now it is reviewed and revised at the end of every year with the teaching assistants. The first two pages are not about the personal being political, or about how this course is going to change the world. They are filled with rules that I the undisputed authority have set down for students: They are to come on time; they are not to leave early or start to pack up their things five minutes before the end of class; they are not to read the newspaper or talk to their neighbor during class; they are not to cheat and if they do, we will fail them; they are not to get airline tickets before the final exam schedule is printed because having such tickets is not an acceptable excuse for missing the final; attendance will be taken in the thirty-person sections they are required to attend and if they do not come, they will lose points on their grades.

I don't feel like an ogre, nor do I think I have been co-opted. Students enroll in this class from all parts of the university: from the schools of business and health sciences as well as social and behavioral sciences and humanities and fine arts; majors in wood technology and engineering as well as English and history. Some students are in the Greek system; others are athletes; twenty percent are men. Not all have enrolled because of an interest in women's issues, though that is true for some. Most students are here because this course fulfills two university requirements: an "I" for "interdisciplinary" and a "D" for "diversity," and only few courses of this sort exist.

Five teaching assistants each lead two sections of thirty; ten sections. Six hundred students a year will be able to fulfill the "D" and "I" requirements by taking WOST 187. The teaching assistants are advanced graduate students in various departments, since women's studies has been unable to implement the graduate certificate program approved by the university years ago. We do not have enough faculty in the department and there has been no money to hire more. Most teaching assistants work two jobs to support themselves and sometimes children. All of their dissertations are focused on women's issues. The success of this course depends heavily on these women who lead the weekly discussion sections and deal with the fallout from my lectures: the anger, the resistance, the hostility, and eventually the learning and the growth.

There is still a low rumble in the room and I prepare to assert my authority. I tell the students to find seats and be quiet. Then I read the rules from the syllabus because I know that no matter how many times during the semester I tell them to read the syllabus, some of them will not. I want to be clear. They are quiet now. Some look resentful as they hear the authority in my voice and look at the hefty syllabus, having perhaps expected a "gut" course. Others look expectant, waiting for me to get to the "woman" part. I ask who they think about when I say "woman" or "women?" A few courageous students tentatively raise their hands. After the first few speakers, more hands go up and students call the names of the significant women in their lives: their mothers, grandmothers, sisters, teachers, neighbors. I listen attentively and repeat what they have said for those who did not hear. When I see no more hands, I look at the mostly European-American students and ask if the women they named or thought about look like themselves? Are they the same color? Class? Sexuality? Slowly, most of the students who spoke nod their heads in assent. I begin the enormously difficult tasks I will be engaged in all semester: to both validate their experience and broaden their vision; to provide an analysis which looks at both the similarities and the differences in women's lives; to establish that women's lives are worthy of study, that gender is an important category of analysis, that women's lives are shaped by patriarchal institutions even while some women are in power over other women, and even some men, and that some women gain privilege through the oppression of other women. I contextualize gender, not privilege it, so that women's lives are understood through an analysis which integrates gender with race, class, and sexuality. And I must do this in fifty-minute lectures to three hundred students, 90 to 95 percent of whom tell us that they are not feminists in the survey we administer at the beginning and end of each semester.

I point out that their conceptualization of women has drawn only on their own experiences and has been individualized. I tell them that both are important, expressing the idea that the personal is political, but not yet using the words which will be part of the lecture on the history of the women's movement. But I go on to say that we have to be aware of our assumptions and their effects. Most students are now taking notes as I construct and deconstruct gender. As 11:00 approaches, I end the lecture with a sentence or two about the next class which will focus on Columbus's invasion of the ancient land that came to be called the "New World." I put down the microphone and the room fills with the sounds of three hundred people collecting their things and getting up out of their seats. The teaching assistants and I are surrounded by students, most of whom are trying to get into the class. They know it is closed, but they try to insert humanity into the now computerized registration system. We cannot accommodate them. I cannot overburden the teaching assistants with more than thirty students in their sections. We have ordered only three hundred books and copied only three hundred readers. We are bound by the numbers.

Women's Studies 187 is not what we had imagined in our future twenty years ago, but perhaps our vision was limited by the margins we were on in the 1970s. Perhaps we did not have the courage then to take on the teaching of students who were part of the mainstream. I now see Women's Studies 187 as an opportunity to reach beyond that small circle of feminists to a wide variety of students. They come to fulfill a requirement and I provoke them to think critically about their world, and as we witness the frightening rise of the radical right, the capitulation of the center and the disarray of the left, WOST 187 has become more and more important. At its best, the course provides an important critique of the sexism, racism, classism, and heterosexism that shape our lives and exposes students to the political movements that have changed the world. At the very least, it teaches students some things about women's lives which they will not learn elsewhere. Faced with the discrepancy between what they learned in this class and what they were taught in high school and what they hear and see in the media, students might begin to question the notion of objectivity and begin to understand that getting reliable information is hard work.

A few students will have been so touched by this course that they will become women's studies majors and sit in a circle in classes where, I hope, they will continue to learn about gender as it intersects with race, class, and sexuality. A few others might take more courses in women's studies or look for other courses with a critical perspective on our world. Maybe some students will get involved in progressive activism outside the classroom. Maybe something we do in WOST 187 will plant a seed in some students that will grow into a rage at injustice and maybe they will be empowered enough by their new knowledge of current and past struggles to think that they can change the world. I face the 300 students in this auditorium on the first day of the semester and I think to myself that I have only fourteen weeks to try to challenge these young minds.

ARLENE VOSKI AVAKIAN is on the women's studies faculty at the University of Massachusetts/Amherst. She is author of the memoir *Lion Woman's Legacy* (The Feminist Press, 1992).

Girl

Maureen Brady

IN 1969 I STRETCHED AND STRAINED TO REACH FOR MY OWN POWER BY CALLING MYSELF AND ALL OTHER ADULT FEMALES "WOMEN." I FOUGHT MY BOSS, MY DENTIST, MY GIRLFRIENDS, AND MY MOTHER ON THIS. ALL THOSE TERMS—GIRLS, GALS, LADIES, HENS, CHICKS, BITCHES—WERE DIMINISHING US IN SOME WAY. MY MOTHER COMPLAINED: "BUT IT'S A LIFELONG HABIT FOR ME TO SAY, 'I'M GOING TO MEET WITH THE GIRLS IN MY SEWING CIRCLE TONIGHT.'" I DON'T THINK SHE CONVERTED, LANGUAGE-WISE, BUT WITHIN THE YEAR SHE DID MAKE ME A NEEDLEPOINT SAMPLER (STITCHED IN HER SEWING CIRCLE) WHICH READ: "A WOMAN'S PLACE IS IN THE WORLD." WHEREVER I LIVE, I KEEP IT ON MY KITCHEN WALL.

In 1994, at the Dyke March of Stonewall 25, meeting up with old friends long active as feminists, we greet each other: "Hey girl, how're you doing?" "Girl" has become a nickname for a woman whole unto herself. This was once the meaning of "virgin." I am awed, humbled, and somewhat perplexed by the passage of time and perspective. We have more breathing room now. More room for nuance, which gives us fuller dimensions. That we created this room is a good thing to appreciate and remember.

MAUREEN BRADY is an author whose books include *Give Me Your Good Ear*, *The Question She Put to Herself*, *Midlife: Meditations for Women*, *Daybreak*, and *Folly* (The Feminist Press, 1994).

Photo by Yonah Afia.

Barbie, My Liberator

Alida Brill

I GREW UP IN A PLACE OF SAMENESS. ALL WHITE, ALL MIDDLE CLASS, AND PRESUMABLY ALL CHRISTIAN. IN MY CHILDHOOD HOMETOWN OF LAKEWOOD, CALIFORNIA, CONFORMITY WAS NOT DISCUSSED, IT WAS ASSUMED. THERE, IN OUR IDENTICAL LITTLE HOUSES, 17,500 OF THEM ON A SERIES OF STRAIGHT AND FLATLY CARVED OUT STREETS CREATED FROM BEAN FIELDS, THE AMERICAN DREAM WAS SUPPOSED TO FLOURISH. WE WERE THE CHILDREN OF THE 1950S—BABY BOOMERS WHOSE CHILDHOOD DAYS WERE TO BE SHELVED IN ORDERLY PLACES IN A SERIES OF PLANNED COMMUNITIES LIKE LAKEWOOD THROUGHOUT THE UNITED STATES. DADS WORKED, MOMS STAYED HOME, BOYS PLAYED SPORTS, AND GIRLS PLAYED HOUSE WITH THEIR "BABY DOLLS."

My mother's friend made elaborate party favors: it was the manner in which she made a living. When I was ten years old she gave me a beautifully decorated sugar egg, which had a peep hole at the end of the egg into which you gazed at the interior panorama. Inside the egg were tiny rows of houses, all perfectly decorated in pale colors. There were equally tiny sugar trees and flowers and sugar picket fences. In front of each house was a rabbit family. That was Lakewood to me, a planned town, encased inside the sugary notion that, joined and bounded by regularity, by conformity, by sameness, by whiteness, all the little rabbit families would live happily ever after. And each would do her rabbit best to produce more families to fill the sugar egg.

A sugar egg has no exit and no horizon beyond its sugar egg ceiling. Why should it? Everything could be contained within it—home, family, beauty, happiness: that was what the 1950s symbolized. It was a kind of comfort, a certain predictable life, and the boundaries were safe. For me to stay I would have had to become a sugar rabbit too. After all, that's what little girls are made of—"sugar and spice...." I suspected pretty early that I had neither the desire nor the ingredients to be a sugar rabbit. When our family would take the Red Car downtown, I would bravely think about living a life in Los Angeles. Cities were places of fantasy, places with endless versions of dress-up and make-believe, and a wondrous population of people who did not all act and look the same. I wanted to live in a real city.

When Disneyland opened, other girls loved the Sleeping Beauty Castle and the Fantasyland which adjoined it. I loved Main Street—its pretend streets, reconstructed nineteenth-century horse-drawn "taxi" carriages, and replica sidewalk cafes. When I was eleven, a "Home of the Future" exhibit opened in the Lakewood Shopping Center. I did not want to be in the house of the future; nor did I get a thrill out of walking through Disneyland's Monsanto Home of the Future. I wanted a different future. At least I did until my self-esteem hit the skids, and I moped around waiting to be chosen by a Lakewood boy so I could stay forever. Until that time, I wanted to break out of the mold. When my friends wanted to "play house," I ran home. Why should I play house in the backyard playhouses in the neighborhood? All of Lakewood was playing house. I would do almost anything to amuse myself but I would not play house. I refused. I had a reputation as the little girl who would not play house. My notoriety was such that a younger neighbor would wince when she saw me enter a backyard. "Oh no, here she comes. Now we can't play house."

My best friend was a girl named Kathy Foy and she did not have the makings of a sugar rabbit mommy either. We plotted our escape in one major way. We played with our Barbie dolls just as much as we could possibly get away with. Barbie is now a criminal. She is celebrating her thirty-fifth birthday under serious cloud cover. She has been found guilty by the politically correct police; she is an inappropriate toy for young girls. Barbie has been accused of contributing to the increasing numbers of young girls suffering from anorexia and other eating disorders. She has become the plastic doll version of the flesh-and-bones, ultra-thin super model Kate Moss. It is believed both Barbie and Kate Moss are a bad influence on girls. Barbie is charged with inculcating bad values. Yet, for two Lakewood girls of the 1950s, Barbie represented something else. She represented a non-material model of womanhood.

We were ten years old when she came into existence, just Barbie, there was no Skipper, no Midge, no fancy cars and dream houses or the other mountains of plastic junk created for her in the intervening years. Barbie was a solo act—a doll that was a woman and not a baby. Sitting on Kathy's upper bunk bed, we invented lives and situations for our Barbies. We did not focus on her glamorous body shape. What we cared about was that Barbie could get dressed up and go some place. Kathy could draw, design, and sew, and she made elaborate outfits for our Barbies, as we could not afford the regular Mattel-issue Barbie clothes. When we decided what we wanted our Barbies to be, and to do, and where they were to go, Kathy would lay out the appropriate wardrobes for their independent lives. She said she was going to be a fashion designer; I thought she was brilliant. (She went to graduate school and became a public health professional.)

Despite the utter political incorrectness of this statement, I cannot help but believe our Barbies saved us. No, I don't believe it; I know it. Barbie was our liberator. Safely alone with the dolls, we were in charge of the fantasy, and our fantasies did not match our Ozzie and Harriet surroundings. With our Barbies we could dream about something other than getting married and having children; through our Barbies, we took on opportunities of a wider realm. In the town where practically every mom stayed home, and where all the women were moms, Barbie's initial pre-feminist appearance signaled for us the universe of other possibilities. Gone from our agenda were the eternal rounds of playing mommy and baby doll, complete with baby carriages and strollers tailor-made for child-sized moms. With Barbie acting for us we could be exciting and interesting women in the world.

When the Ken doll came out, Kathy and I were getting too old for the doll phase, even for Barbie. I was just as glad. I was not all that happy about Ken's intrusion into our fantasy life. Kathy got a Ken right away, and he was better looking than the one my mother was able to track down after the run on the stores which followed his introduction. As far as I was concerned, mine had the wrong hair color. By the time my mother could get to the SavOn Drugstore, in the shopping center, there was only one Ken doll left. He had a slight nick out of his fuzzy felt blonde hair. I did take him, flaw and all. I took him but I did not love him, and neither did Barbie. For years my mother insisted on putting Ken and Barbie in birthday or anniversary displays. I always moved Ken out of the display. He was not the point, not for me.

He was the point, of course, for most of America. His creation was greeted with an unparalleled consumer excitement. He was a doll-sized embodiment of the dream of being chosen by a man. I had loved Barbie as my liberator from waiting my turn on the conveyor belt of marriage, family, house.

I was in first grade when actress Grace Kelly became Princess Grace, and I wrote her a letter of congratulations. She sent me a thank-you note, with her golden silhouette image as a crowned, married princess in the corner of the envelope. I thought it was the greatest thing that could happen to an American girl. Just a few years later, I used Barbie as my tool to escape the ideas of being a bride or a princess. For a time, at any rate, I was moving in the right direction.

ALIDA BRILL is a political scientist and author of *Nobody's Business: The Paradoxes of Privacy* and the forthcoming *Lost in Lakewood: From Ozzie and Harriet to the Spur Posse—How a Model California Town Ran Wild*. She is editor of *In a Public Voice: A World Anthology of Women in Politics* (The Feminist Press, 1995).

Photo by Susan Wood.

Feminism and the Future of Reading

Rachel M. Brownstein

"ANYBODY MAY BLAME ME WHO LIKES," SAYS JANE EYRE, BEGINNING TO ACCOUNT FOR HER DESIRE AND DISCONTENT, EXPECTING TO BE BLAMED FOR BEING DIFFERENT. AS IT TURNED OUT, SHE WAS RIGHT: EVEN VIRGINIA WOOLF BLAMED HER—AND CHARLOTTE BRONTË—FOR THIS TOO-BALD INVITATION TO HOSTILE CRITICS. I ECHO HER WORDS NOW TO BRACE MYSELF, EXPECTING TO BE HEARD AS A DISSENTING VOICE.

This is my fear for the next twenty-five years of academic feminism in general, and women's studies in particular: that the increasingly urgent accidental pressures of modern life, and the taste for quick takes, struck attitudes, and jargon, combined with the yen for the new and the old addiction to love or applause or belonging or blamelessness, will make it impossible to get any reading done—make it impossible, that is, to give complex literary texts the attention they demand and deserve, to enjoy them and to learn from them how to attend to the equally complex contexts in which they were written and in which they may, if we don't forget how, continue to be read. My fear is that people like me will be out of business—and if that seems like a selfish fear, well, anybody may blame me who likes.

RACHEL M. BROWNSTEIN, professor of English at Brooklyn College and the Graduate Center, CUNY is author of *Becoming a Heroine: Reading about Women in Novels* and *Tragic Muse: Rachel of the Comédie-Française*. She wrote the afterword to Elizabeth Janeway's *Leaving Home* (The Feminist Press, 1987).

Proud of Women

Judith Bruce

THOUGH I CALL MYSELF A FEMINIST BECAUSE OTHERS DO, MY FEMINISM HAS ALWAYS BEEN SO INTEGRAL TO MY BEING THAT IT IS DIFFICULT TO DEFINE IT AS SOMETHING APART FROM MYSELF. I TELL MY DAUGHTERS THAT A FEMINIST IS SOMEONE WHO IS PROUD OF WOMEN.

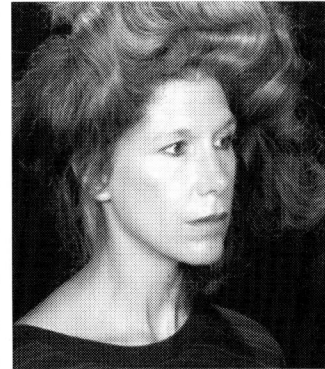

My pride in women has deepened substantially over the last twenty-five years as has my sense of responsibility to the next generation of young women. I feel that young women in all parts of the world between the ages of ten and twenty deserve our special empathy and compassion—it seems to me that there is a systematic devaluation of girls by themselves and by society as their sexual and childbearing capacity arrives. Though nominally celebrated, menarche often exposes young girls to an invasive and uncaring world.

When I began my purposeful/professional work to improve women's access to and control of resources (a field called briefly and unfortunately "Women in Development"), I certainly understood the importance of women having independent income, economic bargaining power, and a range of identities—including economic and community leadership identities. But what I have understood through my work, analysis, and life is that the greatest disadvantage women face has its roots in the special stewardship they feel for children and others. It is women's innate or cultivated sense of responsibility for others, their altruism, their ability to wake up in the morning and give what needs to be given to others that in fact will keep them subjugated. Though I value very much this connection to others, and the world needs it, women's poverty is as much rooted in the burdens of family life on young girls, on young marrieds, on mothers, on adults caring for elders, as in any limits imposed by restricted labor markets and external prejudice. Whereas restructuring women's access to labor markets and public power will be difficult, I believe it will be easy compared to the process of realigning male and female nurturing responsibility.

Apart from the substantive surprises over the last twenty-five years, I feel one very strong emotion: an amazement that we have been able to support each other over these decades. Oftentimes I find myself working in unspoken concert with women I have never met before toward goals and through complexities that require finely tuned strategic vision. But as we are driven by our hearts and not just our heads, our impulses are often magically in sync. I love the quirks of personality and the capacity for outrage and entertainment that characterize so many of the women I work with. There is nothing better than the fierce feminine spirit.

JUDITH BRUCE is a senior associate at the Population Council and director of the Family, Gender, and Development Program in the Council's Programs Division. She has served as project advisor of the SEEDS publication series since its inception, including the books *Seeds: Supporting Women's Work in the Third World* (The Feminist Press, 1989) and *Seeds 2: Supporting Women's Work* (The Feminist Press, 1995), both edited by Ann Leonard.

Beginnings

Urvashi Butalia

WHEN I SAW THE TITLE OF THIS COLLECTION, I WONDERED HOW I COULD "RE-VISION" SOMETHING I HADN'T REALLY "VISIONED." I CAN'T REMEMBER STARTING WITH A VISION OF FEMINISM, OR WAKING UP ONE MORNING AND DECIDING TO BE A FEMINIST. IF I TRY TO THINK BACK TO A BEGINNING, IT SEEMS TO ME THAT I HAVE ALWAYS BEEN HERE, WITH A DEEP SENSE OF THIS BEING HOME AND LIFE. AND YET, STORIES DON'T JUST HAPPEN, THEY HAVE TO BEGIN SOMEWHERE. BUT WHERE? CONSCIOUSLY, SEVERAL WOMEN OF MY GENERATION BECAME FEMINISTS—OR STARTED TO CALL THEMSELVES FEMINISTS—IN OUR UNIVERSITY YEARS WHEN WE HUDDLED TOGETHER IN SMALL GROUPS TO TALK ABOUT THE INJUSTICE OF NOT BEING LET OUT OF OUR HOSTELS AFTER EIGHT AT NIGHT. ONE THING LED TO ANOTHER AND WE FOUND OURSELVES READING FEMINIST TEXTS AND TALKING ABOUT OPPRESSION AND DECIDING THAT WE HAD TO DO SOMETHING. BUT WAS THAT, THEN, THE BEGINNING? OR WAS IT AT HOME, WHEN AS CHILDREN WE WOULD SNEAK INTO THE ROOM WHERE OUR GRANDMOTHER SNORED THROUGH HER AFTERNOON SIESTA, AND STEALTHILY UNTIE THE KEYS TO THE PANTRY FROM THE DRAWSTRING OF HER *SHALVAAR* SO THAT WE COULD EAT ALL THE GOODIES WE'D BEEN DENIED BECAUSE WE WERE GIRLS? OR WAS IT WHEN I HEARD, WITH SURPRISE—WHICH LATER TURNED TO ADMIRATION—MY MOTHER, A MIDDLE-CLASS INDIAN HOUSEWIFE, SAYING TO MY FATHER THAT SHE HATED HOUSEWORK AND REFUSED TO BE FORCED INTO DOING IT JUST BECAUSE SHE WAS A WOMAN?

Many beginnings, across the world, in different cultures, in different lands....Looking back on my own life, perhaps that has been the most important lesson—that if all of us from so many different cultures, regions, geographies, feel there's something to be fought for, then that something must be important. It may be different, individually and collectively, depending on where we come from, who we are, what our color is, how we define our sexuality, but it's there. At times I have felt daunted by its magnitude—how could we have taken on such a profoundly difficult task? Are we equal to it? At other times, I am reassured by our foolhardiness: If we've been silly enough to take this on, it must have something in it, it must be right. And if today, a woman from India and a woman from Africa can strike up an immediate rapport, even without language in common, then we must be pretty special indeed.

For me personally, feminism has led to an involvement in feminist publishing and has enabled me to combine a professional capability with a political commitment and a personal interest. Who could be so lucky? And who'd want to re-vision that?

URVASHI BUTALIA is copublisher of the Indian publishing house Kali for Women. She is an editor of *Truth Tales: Contemporary Stories by Women Writers of India* (The Feminist Press, 1990) and *Slate of Life: More Contemporary Stories by Women Writers of India* (The Feminist Press, 1994), both originally published by Kali for Women.

Hard to Imagine

Mariam K. Chamberlain

IT'S HARD FOR ME TO IMAGINE WHAT WOMEN'S STUDIES WOULD BE LIKE WITHOUT THE FEMINIST PRESS.

MARIAM K. CHAMBERLAIN is founding president of The National Council for Research on Women and coeditor with Liza Fiol-Matta of *Women of Color and the Multicultural Curriculum* (The Feminist Press, 1994).

Re-Visioning Feminism in a Post-Apartheid South Africa

Jacklyn Cock

CONTEMPORARY SOUTH AFRICA RAISES IMPORTANT QUESTIONS REGARDING BOTH THE LIMITS AND THE POSSIBILITIES OF FEMINIST STRUGGLE. IN MAIDS AND MADAMS, I MAINTAINED THAT THE EXPLOITATIVE NATURE OF RELATIONSHIPS BETWEEN BLACK AND WHITE WOMEN MEANT THAT SOUTH AFRICA PRESENTED A CHALLENGE TO ANY SIMPLE FEMINIST NOTION OF "SISTERHOOD." HOWEVER, FOURTEEN YEARS LATER THE SOUTH AFRICAN TRANSITION FROM APARTHEID TO DEMOCRACY HAS INCLUDED AN INSPIRATIONAL EXAMPLE OF WOMEN'S UNITY. THIS UNITY TOOK ORGANIZATIONAL FORM IN THE WOMEN'S NATIONAL COALITION (WNC), AN ALLIANCE OF ALMOST ONE HUNDRED DIFFERENT ORGANIZATIONS OF WOMEN, FORMED IN 1992 TO IDENTIFY AND CODIFY WOMEN'S NEEDS AND ASPIRATIONS IN "A WOMEN'S CHARTER," A PROCESS COMPLETED IN 1994.

This charter clearly acknowledges the differences among South African women. The Women's National Coalition attempts to develop a political practice which incorporates and builds supportive alliances based on these differences. The notion of "coalition politics" avoids political fragmentation or forcing a false universalism onto the women's movement. Instead it allows for both autonomous organization and actions as well as cooperation and coordinated programs for greater impact. Largely due to the activities of this organization, South African women have made impressive gains. There has been a reconfiguration of the discourse on gender and a dramatic increase in the number of women in parliament. South Africa has moved from 141st on the list of countries with women in parliament to seventh. We have 106 women in parliament, a woman speaker, and two women cabinet ministers (out of thirty) in the Government of National Unity.

Will these women parliamentarians act differently from men? Will they create a different political culture, adopt a different style of political behavior, and identify a different set of priorities? The answer lies partly, I believe, in moving beyond a narrow and exclusive focus on "women's issues" to analyze all issues in terms of a gender lens. The traditional feminist focus on women's issues such as child care, maternity leave, sexual harassment, and so on leaves untouched too many institutions which structure access to power and resources in society, especially the arms trade and control of the military.

The arms industry in South Africa is planning to treble arms exports by the end of 1998. This is generating little protest although the horrors of war are evident in the television coverage of Rwanda, a country the South African arms industry admits to having supplied with weapons in 1991. Feminists all over the world need to unite to oppose this misuse of human resources.

The United Nations meetings in Rio and Vienna were important signposts for such a global transformation agenda on environmental and feminist issues. But this analysis needs to be balanced by the appreciation of the social meanings attached to both "nature" and "women" in indigenous cultures. Both environmentalism and feminism are, to some extent, discredited in the South—environmentalism for its narrow focus on "conservation," rather than on health and development issues; feminism for its alleged divisiveness in struggles of national liberation.

In the future, the transformative potential of feminism depends on an appreciation of "difference" and a sensitivity to the contextual and local. These emphases on "difference" and "context" are central themes of an emerging postmodernist feminism. However, the postmodernist feminist literature is increasingly elitist, and accessible only to that small minority of women privileged to have had an epistemological training. Instead we need to construct a new feminism to provide us with a political road map whereby we can move beyond taking up short-term, narrow issues and link up with other social movements—particularly the antimilitarism and the environmental movements—to form effective alliances and campaigns. We need to be sensitive to "difference" and "context" but at the same time weave a global solidarity that will deepen our shared understandings of a gendered vision of society, politics, and culture, and develop our collective strength.

JACKLYN COCK is in the department of sociology at the University of Witwatersrand, Johannesburg, South Africa. She is working on a revision of Maids and Madams for The Feminist Press and is a consultant for The Press's Women Writing in Africa project.

Photo by Gill de Vlieg

Excerpt From
Conversations: Straight Talk With America's Sister President*

Johnnetta B. Cole

FEMINISM IS QUITE SIMPLY THE ANTIDOTE TO SEXISM. THE FEMINIST MOVEMENT IS BASED ON THE BELIEF THAT MEN AND WOMEN ARE EQUAL AS HUMAN BEINGS. IN OTHER WORDS, NONA IS NOT INEVITABLY THE TYPIST (OR NOW THE "WORD PROCESSOR") AND NICK IS NOT INEVITABLY THE BOSS. FEMINISM INSISTS THAT WOMEN SHOULD RECEIVE EQUAL PAY FOR EQUAL WORK, HAVE DECISION-MAKING POWER WHEN IT COMES TO THEIR OWN BODIES, AND ENJOY THE OPPORTUNITY TO PARTICIPATE FULLY IN THE POLITICAL LIFE OF THEIR COMMUNITIES AND THEIR NATION. FEMINISM PRESUPPOSES THAT WOMEN ARE CAPABLE OF DRIVING CARS WELL, SOLVING COMPLEX MATHEMATICAL PROBLEMS, AND PLAYING THE SAXOPHONE. FEMINISM CHALLENGES THE ASSUMPTION THAT ANY COMPANY OR ORGANIZATION WILL RUN AMUCK BECAUSE IT HAS A WOMAN AT THE HELM.

Feminism contends that although men do not give birth to children, they are quite capable of loving and rearing them because there is nothing that keeps them from being nurturing, caring human beings. Feminism hopes that men, like women, will help sons and daughters with their homework, visit sick relatives in the hospital, and remember Grandma's birthday when it comes around. Feminism shudders at the notion that "real men" don't cry, don't sew buttons, and don't do a thousand and one other things in the bogus category "unmanly."

I am not a betting woman, but I would venture to say that one would have to search high and low to find large numbers of African-American women who disagree with the fundamental goals of feminism. I believe that because of our "adventure" with racism we have a deep and abiding attachment to equality that extends to all dimensions of being. Hence, I think many of us automatically embrace feminism even though we may reject the word. When a woman is angry and says, "I am doing exactly the same job as this guy in my office and doing it just as well, why is he getting more money than I am?" that is a feminist question. (A nonfeminist accepts that she is paid less because she is a woman.) When a woman asks her mate, "What makes you think I am any less tired than you? I worked a full day just like you did. I don't see why you get to sit down, drink beer, and watch a baseball game while I cook dinner, get the children washed, and straighten up the house," that is a feminist talking.

Although many African-American women subscribe to the basic principles of feminism, the truth of the matter is that "feminist" is not a word that sits comfortably with the vast majority of us, nor a movement to which in large numbers we consciously and actively pledge our allegiance. The reasons are multiple; among them, the tactics of antifeminists to discredit the movement, the behavior of some white feminists, and, to some extent, the short-sightedness of African-American women.

African-American women have not escaped the profound homophobia that grips American society. Perhaps the most unspoken but deep-seated fear of many African-American women is that any association with feminism will be construed as evidence of lesbianism.

In addition to the stigma the media attaches to the feminist movement, African-American women's disaffection stems from issues revolving around race and racism. Historically, for most white women "women's liberation" has meant "white women's liberation": So impenetrable was their racism, they were unable to see African-American women as women, too. When they did include us—sometimes out of enlightenment, but often for political expediency—our contributions, interests, and sensibilities were shoved to the periphery if kept in view at all.

Many African-American women approached feminism with suspicion because one of the standard phrases of the women's movement proclaimed that we women are "all sisters!" That pronouncement was often followed by the assertion that raising differences among us is divisive. But as poet Audre Lorde has said: "It is not difference which immobilizes us, but silence. And there are so many silences to be broken." As much as the conditions and experiences of white women, African-American women, and other women of color may be similar, there are very important differences in our circumstance and experiences, differences that defy singular analyses of women's oppression and blanket dictums about how to achieve gender equality.

I am not convinced that the coming of age of African-American women into feminism can be achieved by switching terms, and I certainly see no reason that "feminism" or "feminist" should belong exclusively to white women. Yet, when Alice Walker coined the term "womanist," many of us were attracted to it.

We liked the sound, the feel of "womanist." It struck a chord; it was familiar. Familiar because we remember our mothers, grandmothers, aunts, and other womenfolk pulling our pigtails and chiding us with "Don't come 'round here with those womanly ways of yours," or "You're acting too womanish for me."

If African-American women are able to work in conjunction with other women of color and white women on mutual and separate agendas, there will be more power to the movement. But if in some instances such coalitions are not feasible or productive for African-American women, then there may have to be a temporary parting of ways. Should this occur, we may be accused of splintering the movement, of diluting its potency. There may arise mutterings that we are being "too black" or "getting black all of a sudden." We, of course, will know that we have been black for a very long time. And once again, we must keep on keepin' on, strengthened by the trust in Anna Julia Cooper's oft-quoted declaration: Only the Black Woman can say, "when and where I enter, in the quiet, undisputed dignity of my womanhood, without violence and without suing or special patronage, then and there the whole...*race enters with me.*"

More than anything else, African-American women who are feminists and mothers or guardians must find ways to raise their girls and boys as feminists, too. We are individuals with the greatest power to raise a generation of new women and new men.

This excerpt first appeared in the book Conversations: Straight Talk With America's Sister President, *originally published by Doubleday in 1993.*

JOHNNETTA B. COLE is president of Spelman College. She is author of *Conversations, Anthropology for the Nineties: Introductory Readings, All American Women: Lines That Divide. Ties That Bind*, and she contributed an afterword to *The Changelings* by Jo Sinclair (The Feminist Press, 1985).

Photo by Bud Smith Photo.

The Promise of Feminism

Clare Coss

WHEN FEMINISM CAME INTO MY LIVING ROOM IN THE MID-SIXTIES IN THE PERSON OF LILA KARP, IT GAVE ME A BIG HEADACHE. SHE SPOKE OF HER NEW BOOK, *THE QUEEN IS IN THE GARBAGE*, IN THE FACE OF ARGUMENTS, AMUSEMENT, AND DENIAL FROM THOSE MEN PRESENT AT THE SMALL DINNER PARTY MY HUSBAND AND I HOSTED. WITH EACH WORD I FELT MORE CHALLENGED AND MORE FRIGHTENED. I KNEW TAKING ON THE FIGHT FOR EQUAL RIGHTS WAS GOING TO CHANGE MY LIFE.

Before long I was writing my first published and produced feminist play. In *Titty Titty Bang Bang* a woman karate-kicks a path through parental and societal voices designed to limit and constrict her life. As she becomes progressively conscious of patriarchal oppression, a clearing is thrashed open in which she can begin to define and act on priorities and interests designed to liberate herself and other women.

Three decades later I reflected on these beginnings en route to Hawaii for a dream vacation with my partner and goddaughter. Jotted in my notebook were two questions Florence Howe posed for this journal: Has your view of feminism changed in the last twenty-five years? What is important to the future of feminism?

On the plane I read another woman's journey west in a collection called *A Hawaiian Reader*. In 1828 a young missionary woman, Laura Fish Judd, composed her first impression of the islands. "The ship glides along smoothly; the clouds open— the blue space has become a broad mountain; now we see the green valleys and dashing cascades all along the northern shores of the island....Can anything so fair be so defiled by idol worship and deeds of cruelty?"

She and her missionary husband intended to impose their protestant religion, puritan values, and strict behavioral codes on the native women, men, and children. They were trained to obliterate customs, belief systems, cultures they knew nothing about; they were the enemy of the sacred hula. The missionaries did not consider for a moment that they may have had something to learn from the Hawaiians, about themselves, about living in sensual harmony with respect for nature. (There are a thousand kinds of rain that fall on the islands, with a thousand names.)

As I looked down from the plane window on the thick air of Honolulu, on the military vessels in polluted Pearl Harbor, I reflected upon the impact the Judds and the stream of missionaries in league with traders and imperialists have had on these beautiful, conquered, militarized islands.

As the three of us embarked on vigorous adventures, sea kayaking out to Captain Cook Point on the Big Island, exploring the night sky through a telescope atop Mauna Kea, hiking the Waimea Canyon on Kauai, I thought about the personal impact feminism has had on my life. That young me attentive in my matrimonial living room never dreamed she would be fit enough someday for the exhilarating athletics of this trip. She never imagined she would allow her heart to seek the deeply satisfying love of a woman. She had yet to march, to speak out, to act, to become part of a movement working on behalf of women's lives. She did not understand the ironclad connection between economics and racism and the roller skates of white/class privilege.

From the vantage point of Hawaii in the mid-nineties, Laura Judd's question turned back on me: "Can anything so fair be defiled by idol worship and deeds of cruelty?" Our brutish and greedy policies objectify Hawaiian women as exotic aloha objects in grass skirts; native Hawaiians, twenty percent of the population, so many of whom are in diaspora, are the dispossessed—the homeless, the unemployed, the imprisoned. Gorgeous birds and flowers and fish have disappeared or are endangered. Sailing to the Na Pali coast to swim and snorkel with giant sea turtles, the captain points out U.S. missile installations on sacred land, the silent cliffs bereft of once profuse and brilliant bird flocks.

On the plane home—refreshed, invigorated, and profoundly informed—I struggled with the contradictions of a dream vacation built on what is for so many Hawaiians a nightmare reality. I turned to Haunani Kay Trask's book, *From a Native Daughter*. Trask, a leader in the Hawaiian sovereignty movement, is explosive and specific: "At this point in our struggle, race and culture are stronger forces than sex and gender....Haole [white] feminists have steadfastly refused to support our efforts to regain our lands, to protect our civil rights, and to achieve self-government." Trask powerfully illustrates the many ways her people organize to survive the tidal wave of tourists, "uninvited guests," and struggle against the threat of their own "planned disappearance."

When I see through wide open feminist eyes, everything looks different. There is no escape from responsibility. Anger and grief and hope interlock into a wellspring of action.

For me the future of feminism depends on our continuing to learn about the complex conditions for survival, dignity, and justice across the globe. Feminism opens the possibility to join in solidarity with movements that stand for freedom in the fight against prejudice, racism, fundamentalism, and economic predators at home and abroad. Just as feminism strengthens me, informs my work as a psychotherapist and playwright, gives me the gifts of love, activism, and community, it holds vast promise for every woman.

CLARE COSS is a playwright, psychotherapist, and activist. Her play *Lillian Wald: At Home on Henry Street*, **produced at the New Federal Theater (NYC), is included in the book she edited,** *Lillian Wald: Progressive Activist* **(The Feminist Press, 1989).**

Photo by Virginia Fox.

A Long Way to Go

Margaret Cruikshank

FEMINISM CHANGED MY LIFE. I AM NOT AS SINGLE-MINDEDLY FOCUSED ON IT AS I WAS IN THE 1970S, BUT I REMAIN STAUNCH. WHEN I TAUGHT MY FIRST WOMEN'S STUDIES COURSE IN 1975, RELATIVELY FEW WOMEN DID THIS WORK. NOW WE ARE THOUSANDS. FOR THE FIRST TIME, IN 1995, THE ENGLISH DEPARTMENT OF THE CITY COLLEGE OF SAN FRANCISCO WILL OFFER A WOMEN'S STUDIES IA (FRESHMAN COMPOSITION) COURSE. THIS IS A SIGN THAT FEMINIST THINKING AND TEACHING ARE STILL FILTERING INTO THE TRADITIONAL CURRICULUM. WE HAVE A LONG WAY TO GO, OF COURSE, UNTIL THE CAMPUS IS A COMPLETELY HOSPITABLE ENVIRONMENT FOR WOMEN.

MARGARET CRUIKSHANK teaches English and lesbian/gay studies at the City College of San Francisco and is editor of the first edition of *Lesbian Studies: Present and Future* **(The Feminist Press, 1982).**

Photo by Barbara Giles.

For My Granddaughter

Doris Groshen Daniels

I DON'T REMEMBER WHICH CAME FIRST—MY INTEREST IN THE FEMINIST MOVEMENT OR MY CONCENTRATION IN THE STUDY AND TEACHING OF WOMEN'S HISTORY—BUT BOTH WERE A PART OF THE WAVE OF REFORMIST IDEALISM THAT MADE POSSIBLE INSTI-TUTIONS LIKE THE FEMINIST PRESS. DESPITE THE PROBLEMS AND OBSTACLES, I FULLY EXPECTED THAT THE ACTIVISM OF THE TIME WOULD MAKE THE LIVES OF MY YOUNG DAUGH-TERS VASTLY DIFFERENT FROM MINE.

In part, my hopes have been realized. This generation of women has greater career choices, greater freedom, and higher goals than mine did. But, at times, it seems that the idea of true equality is under constant attack and that no victory is ever secure.

Today, I am less naive than I was twenty-five years ago, but the idealism that attracted me to the cause originally makes me feel that women's equality may still be realized, if not for me or my daughters then for my granddaughter. Allow me to start the campaign early. Kayla (Daniels) Blackborow for president in 2040!

DORIS GROSHEN DANIELS, professor of history and political science at Nassau Community College, is author of *Always a Sister: The Feminism of Lillian D. Wald* (The Feminist Press, 1989).

Photo by Shepperd Daniels.

The Bonds of Sisterhood

Barbara Ehrenreich and Deirdre English

BESIDES THE EXCITEMENT OF TELLING UNTOLD STORIES, TWO DICHOTOMIES WERE IN OUR MINDS WHEN WE WROTE *WITCHES, MIDWIVES AND NURSES: A HISTORY OF WOMEN HEALERS* AND *COMPLAINTS AND DISORDERS: THE SEXUAL POLITICS OF SICKNESS*. ONE WAS THAT BETWEEN WOMAN-AS-VICTIMIZED VERSUS WOMAN-AS-POWERFUL. THE OTHER WAS BETWEEN THE VISION OF WOMEN AS UNITED BY SEX VERSUS WOMEN BEING DIVIDED BY CLASS.

The first sentence of *Witches* is "Women have always been healers." It is a history of how women's strength as nurturers, nurses, herbalists, midwives, and medical practitioners was usurped by forces, from the Inquisition to the A.M.A., that found them threatening. What happened to witches remains a cautionary tale about how it is often the resister, not the succumber, who gets victimized. Today there is much trendy talk of "victim-feminism"; neo-feminist conservatives accuse the women's movement of "whining."

But whining is the pastime of the weak. Protest is the chosen method of the strong—yet protesters are forever re-victimized, keeping the vicious circle in rotation. After twenty-five years of feminism, it is obvious that women are strong—and that feminism celebrates women's strength, not their victimization.

It is also obvious that the high price strong women pay for seeking or taking power is a defining way that women feel the backlash, from witches to "bitches." But if pushing for equality is still a risky business for women, so much the more reason for women to band together with one another for inspiration, sanity, and support.

In the second pamphlet, *Complaints and Disorders*, we were considering the feminist argument that all women are bonded by their common oppression against the equally convincing leftist argument that women are divided against one another by allegiances or dependencies on the men of their own class. It was particularly instructive to see how both upper-class and lower-class women were harmed by sexism, but in different ways.

Upper-class women were told by doctors that they were the weaker sex, and dare to go to college, because education would deform the uterus. Factory women and domestic servants, in contrast, were considered by scientists to be lower on the evolutionary scale—hence able to work brutally long days without breaks. Looking at such incongruities, so irrational in hindsight, helped to illustrate that much of what we think is "natural" is actually—an exciting new term to us then—"socially constructed."

We hoped that examining women's class differences in the context of overwhelming sexual discrimination against all women would help add to feminism a sense of practical class consciousness. It was already clear to many that the women's movement would tend to be dominated by the interests of middle-class white women, and that in turn would alienate the working class from the movement. What was needed, then as now, was an awareness that feminism would require an understanding of women's differences as well as their similarities.

Twenty-five years later, what do we see? On one hand, the media has promoted the image of a white, middle-class, professionalized feminism—the well-known superwoman. The public response to this narrowed vision is unsurprisingly fickle—it's trendy today, passé tomorrow. Beyond that picture, and sadly under-reported, is the fact that working-class women are as likely as professional women to want a strong women's movement—and black women are committed to feminist goals in greater percentages than white women. To its credit, the ideology of the organized women's movement, never as racist, elitist, or nativist as the nineteenth-century version was, has fought for the rights of women in all classes and has avoided pitting women of different classes against each other.

But the American economy *has* pitted women against one another according to the diverging interests of diverging classes. It was never feminism which "drove women to the workplace"—feminism has always touted the idea of choice, and has rarely derogated motherhood. But the declining real wages of American households did push women into the work force (where feminist organizing, litigation, and legislation helped improve their conditions and pay, relative to male workers). Working women, providing second incomes, are the heroes of the American status quo, such as it has been—the reason that the majority of families did not fall into poverty over the last twenty-five years.

What this means is that women swept into the work force and received virtually no economic gain for their families or, to speak collectively, their sex, except for the upper middle class. Out of that class, the only thing that makes it easier to combine work and motherhood is the fact that women have had enough reproductive rights to have reduced the average number of children they bear, as well as to have controlled the timing of their births. Outside of the upper middle class, it is no easier to prosper as a single woman or to survive on a woman's paycheck or support a family without a second breadwinner.

Working women's extraordinary contribution to the American economy and the maintenance of family stability has never been adequately acknowledged or appreciated because women's "double duty" was handily attributed to a self-selected "liberation." This is in no way meant to contradict the fact that most women are glad they went to work—for their family, and for themselves, and for the increased status and pride they so clearly feel.

But the economic shakedown continues. And increasingly women (and feminism) are taking the blame for the breakdown of the family, and the other signs of an economy that cannot provide what it once did. Blame the victim, once again! Economic polarization widens, and women are more separated by a class divide than ever since the post-war period began. Now the neo-feminist conservatives ride in again to say that middle-class women should vote against the poor, who are mostly women and children. And what does the true-blue feminist say?

What's needed is a resurgence of the bond of sisterhood, of the notion that what is said about lazy welfare mothers, "illegitimate" children, promiscuous teenagers and so forth is a reintroduction of sexist language which demeans all women. A feminism that can celebrate the gains of the middle-class professional woman without apology, yet not forget the majority of women for whom everyday sexism and class oppression may be every bit as onerous as they were decades ago. As the social and economic differences between women gape wider, the collective consciousness which is the very basis of feminism, and which has provided women with stunning victories this century, is threatened again.

BARBARA EHRENREICH is a political essayist, columnist, social critic, and author of numerous books, including *Fear of Falling* and *Kipper's Game*. DEIRDRE ENGLISH (shown) is a public affairs commentator on San Francisco public radio and television, and former executive editor of *Mother Jones*. They coauthored *Complaints and Disorders: The Sexual Politics of Sickness* (The Feminist Press, 1973), *Witches, Midwives, and Nurses: A History of Women Healers* (The Feminist Press, 1973), and *For Her Own Good: 150 Years of the Experts' Advice to Women*.

Economic Security and the Future of Feminism

Elizabeth Freilicher

MUCH HAS CHANGED FOR WOMEN DURING MY LIFETIME (I AM 86), BUT STILL MUCH HAS TO BE DONE. THERE ARE MORE WOMEN IN THE PROFESSIONS, ON COLLEGE CAMPUSES, IN EXECUTIVE POSITIONS IN INDUSTRY, IN THE SCIENCES, IN ALL LEVELS OF GOVERNMENT, IN NONTRADITIONAL JOBS, IN THE ARMED FORCES, EVEN IN SPACE. BUT THE POOR HAVE NOT BENEFITTED FROM THE ADVANCES THAT MIDDLE-CLASS WOMEN AND WEALTHY WOMEN HAVE MADE.

Women and children constitute a large portion of poor Americans. The women work because they must help house and feed their families. They work at menial jobs. They do not have economic equity, quality child care, upward mobility, or decent health care. And they do not have the strength or time to participate in the political process and work for the change they deserve. They are politically powerless and the only way to involve them in the political process is to give them economic security.

I visualize a future for feminism in which women, and men too, will mobilize their forces to fight for economic security for all. Feminism will no longer be a gender movement. It will be a movement for humanism. After all, feminism was born of humanism.

ELIZABETH FREILICHER is a poet, prizewinning writer, and director of children's radio drama. She is coauthor with Hilda E. Wenner of *Here's to the Women: 100 Songs for and about American Women* (The Feminist Press, 1991).

Teaching in Japan

Kumiko Fujimura-Fanselow

SIX YEARS AGO I CAME TO JAPAN TO TEACH WOMEN'S STUDIES AT A NEWLY ESTABLISHED WOMEN'S UNIVERSITY IN YOKOHAMA, NEAR TOKYO. I WAS BORN IN JAPAN AND LIVED HERE UNTIL THE AGE OF EIGHT, WHEN MY FATHER TOOK A LEAVE FROM HIS COMPANY TO STUDY IN THE UNITED STATES AND OUR FAMILY MOVED THERE. ALTHOUGH I HAD REGULARLY RETURNED TO JAPAN FOR SUMMER VISITS AND TO CONDUCT RESEARCH, THE PAST SIX YEARS HAVE BEEN THE LONGEST TIME I'VE SPENT HERE SINCE I WAS A CHILD. IN ADDITION TO A NUMBER OF FAMILY-RELATED REASONS, A MAJOR ATTRACTION FOR ME IN COMING HERE TO TEACH WAS THE OPPORTUNITY TO INTRODUCE YOUNG JAPANESE WOMEN TO WOMEN'S STUDIES, STILL A RELATIVELY NEW FIELD HERE. I HOPED THAT I COULD HAVE SOME POSITIVE IMPACT GETTING YOUNG WOMEN TO CHALLENGE COMMONLY ACCEPTED VIEWS ABOUT HOW WOMEN SHOULD OR SHOULDN'T BE OR WHAT THEY ARE OR AREN'T CAPABLE OF ACHIEVING IN JAPANESE SOCIETY AND TO ENVISION A WIDER RANGE OF POSSIBILITIES FOR THEIR LIVES.

Students often ask me, "How did you come to be a feminist and to be interested in teaching women's studies?" In response, I often relate my vivid recollection of a day when I was eleven years old (which would have been about 1958) when a question popped into my mind: Why did my mother take my father's name when she married, and why does such a practice exist? I decided that it didn't make any sense and that if I married I would not take my husband's name. (What in fact happened when I got married was that my husband and I decided to hyphenate our surnames; our two daughters have also been given our hyphenated surname.) This was, I think, just one manifestation of my habit of questioning and doubting, my need to understand "why?" or "why not?" and an unwillingness to accept or go along with something unless I was convinced that it was right or good—in a word, all those things that are essential, in my view, to the making of a feminist.

Further reflection on the question has led me to realize that my mother has also been a major influence. Born in Japan in 1916, my mother had been brought up in a society where opportunities for education beyond elementary school were severely limited, especially for women. Fortunately she was able to receive training in design, which enabled her to obtain a relatively well-paying job with a department store for a few years following her schooling. The single life was not, however, an economically viable or socially acceptable lifestyle for most women in those days, and like so many young women of her generation, she dutifully married at the age of twenty-two a man her parents decided would be an appropriate husband for her. With her obvious intelligence, she might have done more than lived her life as a wife and mother, I sensed, had she been born thirty years later. Her constant admonition to me was to get a good education so that I could be financially independent and do whatever I wanted.

The young women I teach are my older daughter's age. The fact that they are studying at a four-year university is something the majority take for granted, not knowing about their grandmothers and mothers who were denied the opportunity, not realizing that even today women like themselves make up only twenty percent of all female high school graduates. Their previous schooling, in most cases, has not instilled in them the habit of questioning, of turning things over in their minds and raising objections. Feminist educators like myself, though, who are popping up on more and more college campuses in Japan, are endeavoring to nurture those critical attitudes and habits.

Meanwhile, I see evidence all around me of how much Japanese women of all age groups are clamoring to break out of the confines of their traditionally defined roles and to try to define themselves as individual women and assert their own wants and needs. The rise in the number of women in their late twenties and thirties remaining single and the growing incidence of divorce, especially among women with children who have been married for more than several years, often cited as negative impacts of the influence of (particularly) American feminism, are, more accurately, in my view, natural outgrowths of the educational and economic gains made by women which have given them options they did not have in the past.

A question that many raise is how to balance the rising demands and aspirations of women with competing demands and needs of society and family. Japan has been perceived as a relatively stable society, socially, economically, and politically, and the Japanese themselves tend to pride themselves on maintaining such a society. Overlooked, however, has been the point that this stability has been maintained at a cost that has been paid by women, certainly, and by youngsters, whose education has been subordinated to the goals of maintaining group conformity and the pursuit of academic achievement as defined in very narrow terms. Japan is still in a recession, and even if we can look forward to a recovery, the country will never be as prosperous as it was in the mid-1980s, and many adjustments will have to be made in the coming years. Women's changing attitudes and aspirations toward work, marriage, family, and children are certain to play a vital role in this process.

KUMIKO FUJIMURA-FANSELOW is associate professor of women's studies at Toyo Eiwa Women's College in Tokyo and Yokohama. She has published extensively on Japanese women's education and is coeditor with Atsuko Kameda of *Japanese Women: New Feminist Perspectives on the Past, Present, and Future* (The Feminist Press, 1995).

Feminists Old and Young

Margaret Gillett

I WAS BORN IN THE 1930S AND MY GENERATION OF FEMINISTS MAY HAVE BEEN THE LUCKY ONES. WE HAD SCHOOLING, WE HAD THE VOTE, WE HAD HIGHER EDUCATION AND WE HAD ACCESS TO SOME OF THE PROFESSIONS. WE OWED THIS TO OUR FORE-FEMINISTS, TO THEIR CENTURY OF STRUGGLES FOR FRANCHISE, FOR DECENT WORK, FOR DIGNITY AND, IN CANADA, EVEN FOR FORMAL RECOGNITION THAT WOMEN ARE PERSONS. WE HAD A LOT, BUT WE DIDN'T HAVE IT ALL. FAR TOO MANY OF US WERE STILL PHYSICALLY BEATEN, ECONOMICALLY EXPLOITED, SEXUALLY ABUSED, PSYCHOLOGICALLY DOWNTRODDEN.

Yet, we were the lucky ones who rode the waves of civil rights of the 1960s and 1970s. We had marvelous leaders and spokeswomen—Betty Friedan, Florence Howe, Maya Angelou, Gloria Steinem, bell hooks, Toni Morrison... We had the chance to break some very solid barriers, to re-envision a fair shake for women and to invent a new vocabulary to label the ageless but hitherto unnamed wrongs. We coined "feminine mystique," "sexism," "sexual harassment," and "malestream." We created terms to identify our goals—"women's studies," "gender-neutral language," "unisex," "gender equity"... Our expressions are now safely installed in textbooks and dictionaries as part of the universal English language. We did a lot but we didn't do it all.

Younger feminists of the 1990s have the advantage of what we did. Yet problems of violence and injustice remain and even our very victories may put them off track, causing them misleading complacency. I know many undergraduates who think the struggles are actually over and that they can do anything. So they can—up to a point. Our half of the population still does not have as much power, money, or respect as the other half. Young feminists need to realize that the enemy has become remarkably savvy, has appropriated our language, giving it back to us in lip service and hollow rhetoric. Young feminists may not readily see how cunningly camouflaged the traps have become.

But luckily, we are still here—getting wiser, tougher, stronger, and angrier as we get older. We are ready to share what we have learned and to cheer on today's young feminists as they join in the struggle to make things better for all of us and their daughters.

MARGARET GILLETT is Macdonald Professor of Education at McGill University, Canada, and contributed a profile of Maud E. Abbott to *Lone Voyagers: Academic Women in Coeducational Institutions, 1870-1937*, edited by Geraldine Jonçich Clifford (The Feminist Press, 1989).

Photo by Aventure Studio, Montreal, Canada

Letter to Charlotte Perkins Gilman

Catherine Golden

DEAR CHARLOTTE,

I SOMETIMES WONDER WHAT FEMINISM WOULD BE LIKE—AND HOW LESS DEMANDING MY LIFE AS A PROFESSIONAL WOMAN WITH CHILDREN WOULD BE—IF PEOPLE AT THE TURN OF THE CENTURY HAD IMPLEMENTED YOUR IDEAS FOR SOCIALIZING HOUSEHOLD INDUSTRY AND CHILD CARE. DOES IT PLEASE YOU OR DEPRESS YOU THAT *WOMEN AND ECONOMICS* STILL RINGS TRUE FOR FEMINISTS TODAY, GIVEN THAT YOU WROTE IT ALMOST A CENTURY AGO?

We have been friends for a long time now, dear Charlotte, so I feel that I can write frankly. You know how I discovered your ideas when I was in my twenties, and I edited my book about your landmark story *The Yellow Wallpaper* before I became a mother. But, now that I am the mother of adorable but active three-year-old twin boys and an English professor approaching forty, I must confess that I read and relate to your work in a more emphatic, personal way. I still have a kitchen in my home and sometimes I feel like a short order cook, serving "The Holy Stove," as you call it in one of your poems. Child care is not socialized in our society as you envisioned, but it is readily available, so a woman can be a "world-servant instead of a house-servant" and economically free. With several days a week of child care, I am able to juggle marriage and motherhood and also to do some of my professional work, though less than I would like. I don't need to tell you about the challenges of the first year of motherhood. I was oddly comforted by reading in your autobiography how you crawled under beds and into remote closets to hide from the pressures of one baby—can you imagine two? I have a helpful husband who is receptive to feminist ideas; he is the opposite of the narrator's impossible husband, John, in *The Yellow Wallpaper*. Nevertheless, we were so tired that first year that even a "rest cure" like the one you took and hated began to sound appealing. Sleep deprivation and not having time to do my professional work have been the hardest parts of motherhood for me. I adore my children and could not imagine life without them. But it is hard to have your children with you "all the time" as that nerve specialist S. Weir Mitchell had the nerve to recommend to you. Of course, he also told you not to touch pen and pencil as long as you lived, and thank goodness you never listened. You were right when you said in *Women and Economics* that a mother "will love her child as well, perhaps better, when she is not in hourly contact with it, when she goes from its life to her own life, and back from her own life to its life, with ever new delight and power." I miss my children the days they go to child care; working outside the home, I return to my boys refreshed, invigorated from the professional work I trained for. I feel fortunate to have a sphere of my life which is separate from my children, husband, home.

At the turn of the century, you predicted more advances for women in the next fifty than in the past five hundred years. Today one can be a professional woman with a family, but it is challenging. Sign me up for one of those kitchenless apartment houses you envisioned, which included a day nursery and kindergarten staffed with well-trained professional nurses and teachers. Alas, society still has a long way to go, and of late I fear we are backsliding, particularly when I listen to my female college students who praise me for having my children in child care only part-time instead of full-time. Women today still sacrifice themselves for their families and the private home, and some elect to do so. The evolution of society is not as simple as you made it seem, particularly when you take race and class issues into consideration, which I fear you did not, dear Charlotte.

Never fear, you are still my favorite feminist. Now don't get mad at me for using that term; I know you never liked it. But as I look to the future of feminism, I look to your works: *Women and Economics, The Home: Its Work and Influence*, and *Concerning Children*. These are books I will continue to assign to my male and female students at Skidmore College. And my sons, as well as my students, will come of age in your company. Your works are among those we need to remember as we look to women's and men's lives in the twenty-first century.

Fondly,
Catherine Golden

CATHERINE GOLDEN is associate professor of English at Skidmore College. She is editor of *The Captive Imagination: A Casebook on "The Yellow Wallpaper"* (The Feminist Press, 1992).

Books

Charlotte Goodman

LIKE MANY BOOK LOVERS, I CAN DATE IMPORTANT EVENTS IN MY LIFE BY RECALLING THE BOOKS I WAS READING AT CERTAIN TIMES: *THE BROTHERS KARAMAZOV* IN 1955, THE SUMMER AFTER I GRADUATED FROM COLLEGE AND ALSO GOT MARRIED; THE COMPLETE WORKS OF MELVILLE WHEN I WAS PREPARING FOR MY DOCTORAL FIELD EXAMS IN 1964, THE YEAR MY THIRD AND LAST CHILD WAS BORN; *THE FEMININE MYSTIQUE*, WHICH I READ WHILE ROCKING HIS BABY CARRIAGE; *THE AWAKENING*, WHEN I WAS AUDITING JUDITH FETTERLEY'S COURSE, "WOMEN AND LITERATURE," IN 1973; *THE YELLOW WALLPAPER* IN 1974 IN PREPARATION FOR MY FIRST YEAR OF COLLEGE TEACHING AT SKIDMORE COLLEGE; *THEIR EYES WERE WATCHING GOD* AND *THE WOMAN WARRIOR* WHEN I TAUGHT MY FIRST COURSE AT SKIDMORE ON WOMEN WRITERS. THE CHANGE IN THE FOCUS OF MY READING OVER TIME, FROM THE WORKS OF MALE TO FEMALE AUTHORS AND FROM NOVELS DESCRIBING THE EXISTENTIAL QUESTS OF MALE PROTAGONISTS TO THE QUESTS OF FEMALE PROTAGONISTS FOR EQUALITY AND AUTONOMY, HAS PROFOUNDLY INFLUENCED MY OWN LIFE. BOOKS BY AND ABOUT WOMEN HAVE ENABLED ME TO SITUATE MY OWN CONFLICTS AND FRUSTRATIONS WITHIN A LARGER CONTEXT, GRADUALLY MAKING IT POSSIBLE FOR ME TO TRANSFORM MYSELF FROM A DISGRUNTLED, HOUSE-BOUND WIFE AND MOTHER INTO A FEMINIST TEACHER AND SCHOLAR.

The books I will probably associate with the summer of 1994 are those Feminist Press publications I have been rereading as I work on revising the afterword I wrote for the first Feminist Press edition of Edith Summers Kelley's *Weeds*, a 1923 female Bildungsroman about a poor Kentucky farm woman, the second edition of which is scheduled to be published by The Feminist Press in the near future. These books include *Daughter of Earth*, *Quest*, *Now in November*, *Writing Red*, and *These Modern Women: Autobiographical Essays from the Twenties*. The last, edited by Elaine Showalter, provides a valuable historical context for another book I read this summer, Christina Hoff Sommers's *Who Stole Feminism: How Women Have Be-*trayed Women. Though I agree with Sommers's insistence that feminist scholars must interpret data accurately, I am outraged by the vitriolic tone of her book and by the way in which her diatribe about the putative inaccuracies of feminist scholarship has been exploited by the media.

The increasingly hostile climate for feminism today is reflected in the publicity given to books like Sommers's, in the growing militancy of "pro-life" and "pro-family" supporters, and in the vilification of those who advocate "political correctness." As Elaine Showalter observes in her introduction to *These Modern Women*, following the passage of the Nineteenth Amendment, the 1920s also witnessed a decline in support for feminism. Showalter reminds us, however, that despite the attacks on feminist goals and a decline of consensus among feminists during the twenties, a feminist agenda not only survived the Depression but emerged with renewed vigor in the sixties and seventies.

Today, my own view of feminism is somewhat more complex than it was thirty years ago, for I now acknowledge how distorting essentialist views of women—or men—can be. However, heartened by the gains women have made over time, I deplore the attacks on feminism that are now being waged in a number of sectors. One of the most effective ways of preventing the erosion of these gains, I believe, is to continue to write, publish, and disseminate books about women's experiences. In "The Ballad of Ladies Lost and Found," which appears in the new edition of the poetry anthology *No More Masks!*, edited by Florence Howe, Marilyn Hacker celebrates some of the precursors of today's feminists, including Margaret Fuller, about whom Hacker writes:

> "'The life, the life, will it never be sweet?'
> She wrote it once; I quote it once again....'"

If, to use a phrase of Wendy Martin's, "we are the stories we tell," then it is imperative for us both to tell our own stories and to "quote" the words of other women. As I think back on the many works by and about women that I have read and taught during the last thirty years, I note that although each life story recorded within these books is shaped by a unique individual during a particular historical period as a member of a given culture, race, and class, these diverse stories also address issues that should be of concern to all women within the global community. The books we read and share with others can help to forge feminist links among women everywhere.

It is impossible for me to predict what advances and retreats from the multiple feminist agendas of the 1990s will occur during the next twenty-five years, nor what gains and losses for women will accrue. However, I believe that just as my reading of works by women has helped to shape my own feminist agenda, so will the stories women continue to publish and circulate play an important role in determining the various agendas of feminists during the decades to come.

CHARLOTTE GOODMAN is professor of English at Skidmore College. She wrote the afterword to *Weeds* by Edith Summers Kelly (The Feminist Press, 1982).

Photo by Publication Office, Skidmore College.

One Necessary Future

Margaret Morganroth Gullette

THE FEMINISMS HAVE NE-GLECTED ONE OF THE EARLIEST MISSIONS OF AMERICAN AND FRENCH FEMINISM, WHICH WAS TO MAKE AGE SALIENT—INEVITABLE AND UNFORGET-TABLE. FEMINISMS' SEARCH FOR INCLUSIVENESS HAS BEGUN TO PUT RACE AND ETHNICITY AND NATIONALITY, CLASS AND SEXUAL ORIENTATION INTO THE CATEGORY OF WHAT I WOULD CALL "OBLIGATORY CONSIDERATIONS."

"Consideration"—inclusiveness—may be the one "obligation" that the feminists can accept. Proudly accept.

Age has been left behind. Too often, feminists omit age in discourses that seem to cry out for it, or include it perfunctorily, or unwillingly repeat the culture's banalities. Even feminist journals and dictionaries pay little attention. Reviewers do not chide writers for omitting age; no framework exists for noticing omissions. Only a few publishers have series that, by putting age in the title, require scholars and theorists to integrate age into the writer's other concerns. Few conferences include age, not to mention concentrate on "age and..." In literature, the Northeast Modern Language Association conference has for years had a session quaintly called "Literary Approaches to Aging," but the MLA has no equivalent. In many disciplines, age appears to be in the situation that "gender" and "race" were in, say, thirty years ago. There's no urgency felt. And in such circumstances, even among women exposed to feminism, age is mystified, cultural interpretations are thin and static, the narratives and categories are left naturalized and their oppressiveness unexposed, the politics of age and aging remain hidden and baneful, the young are trained to reproduce an ageist system without question, and access to our own true feelings and beliefs is impossible. In such circumstances the idea that there might be a general politics of resistance to being aged by culture is not tantalizing but puzzling, almost meaningless.

The very fact that there are women separately doing careful but brilliant work in age studies in many disciplines is practically unknown. We did not have a common rubric until 1993, when I coined the term "age studies" in an essay in *Aging and Gender in Literature: Studies in Creativity*, edited by Anne M. Wyatt-Brown and Janice Rossen. With the publication of that volume, the University Press of Virginia established a new series known as "age studies." Next year, the Center for Twentieth-Century Studies at the University of Wisconsin-Milwaukee will host two funded fellows in age studies.

The term "age studies" invites interdisciplinary learning and collaboration, suggests links with other cultural studies and asks for investigations of parallels with and asks for divergences from the other theories of difference. Age, from this point of view, is a culturally-constructed system that generates life-course narratives, age-related characteristics, age-graded behaviors and feelings, age hierarchies, power and differentials—a system that operates in complex relations with other systems from birth to death in any given culture. It may affect discourse, practices, and institutions as ubiquitously as gender does. As Kathleen Woodward says, sweepingly but truly, the age system inflects and infects "all our formulations of life's events." These are, dare I say, some of the concepts basic to age studies. But no one can say with certainty what is agreed upon and what is contested at this early stage in the development of the approach. We can be sure only that failing to take age into account does extensive harm.

It's too soon to explain the reluctance of feminists in the humanities and elsewhere to use age more consistently and urgently. (Only when a true age push begins, and people begin to reveal their interests, will we begin to get illuminating accounts.) One obvious reason is that many concerned women hastily assumed that "gerontology" would take care of the entire subject of age, implicitly assuming that age only meant stereotypes, discriminations, economic and social biases, and the publication of fiction and criticism about the elderly. But that in itself was an interesting relegation of concern, a proof of the absence of urgency. The fact is that feminists too breathe in the toxins of ageism along with all the other cultural poisons, and, regardless of our ages, we have not immunized ourselves sufficiently against the stereotypes of all the ages, the constructed dread of aging, and even gerontophobia, the three known age-pandemics of our society. My conversations over the years with friends ominously suggest that in private life, where age is concerned, many women unconsciously choose to fight what they would call "nature" rather than social constructions—because this seems to be the easier course. *We are all recovering ageists.* That can be a gloomy observation, but if we begin to know in detail what recovering from ageism involves, it could become a hopeful assertion.

Another explanation for reluctance may be that age complicates the analysis of gender and women, which remain central concepts of feminism. Theory appears to be most successful with an abstract and generalizable subject, and like most theory, much feminist theorizing has not problematized its unmoving subject, a subject that does not "age," a subject that however otherwise understood as constructed, still has no temporality. What age "is" the feminist subject?

Perhaps this is only my deep desire speaking, but my hunch is that the place of age studies will change rapidly in the next ten years in the United States. Now, while the momentum for an ever-increasing inclusiveness still exists, should be one good time to try to raise the consciousness of women in the academy and in the mainstream. The emotional levers of change will not be guilt, but curiosity and self-interest and the allure of the undiscovered, first of all on the part of women who have been in the second wave for decades. And then there will be anger, at the suffering inflicted by the culture, and then a realization that some of it could be avoided. And then, perhaps, resistance, and—the title of my next book—cultural combat.

MARGARET MORGANROTH GULLETTE is author of *Safe at Last in the Middle Years: The Invention of the Midlife Progress Novel*. She also wrote the afterword to Mona Caird's *The Daughters of Danaus* (The Feminist Press, 1989).

Photo by Lilian Kemp Photography.

Something Remembered, Not Exactly Re-Visioned

Anne Halley

Recently I saw *SHLEMIEL THE FIRST*, A MUSICAL BASED ON A PLAY BY ISAAC SINGER. THE PLAYERS WORE LOOSE, EMBLEMATIC COSTUMES WHICH THEY PASSED BE-TWEEN AND AMONG THEM-SELVES AT NEED. ENVELOPES OF GENDER: BLACK CAFTANS FOR MALENESS, VOLUMINOUS PADDED DRESSES WITH SWING-ING HOOP SKIRTS, WIDE HIPS AND WAISTS, POUCHY, LOW POUTER-PIGEON BREASTS FOR FEMININITY. CLEVERLY AND EFFECTIVELY, THE ENVELOPES PASSED AMONG MEMBERS OF THE COMPANY AS THEY SANG AND DANCED: MALE ACTORS CAVORTED IN FEMALE ENVELOPES AND VICE VERSA. THE GEN-DER STEREOTYPES OF DISTANT NINETEENTH-CENTURY YID-DISH SHTETL FOLKLORE STILL AMUSED; THEY TITILLATED AS THEY BECAME RELATIVIZED AND FLUID; THEY DID NOT THREATEN THE CONTEMPORARY AUDIENCE.

In spite of the joyful, raucous drive of *klezmer* music, I could not quite give myself to the experience.

During the shtetl day the women shook and whipped about in their assertive gender armor: quarreling, cooking, berating husbands and children, going to market. The padded armor, however, covered over and hid vulnerable, loving, and simple sexual selves. This was revealed when the central couple, Mr. and Mrs. Shlemiel, lay on their marriage bed and sang to each other. The woman especially seemed slim and girlish, totally other than her daytime self, in white, artfully artless, modest, old-fashioned underclothes.

When Mrs. Shlemiel rose and velcroed her slender self into the heavy dress-body of matron/wife/mother to meet the day, I felt a jolt of panicky protest. Will you (I?) again and again don that flesh, be clothed in those breasts, blood, womb, and the rest of it—carry the weight—every day of my (your?) life? I wanted Mrs. Shlemiel and myself out from under, desperately, and not just for the night.

For a moment the modestly half-dressed figure on stage in knee-length underpants called up a childhood actress-companion, although that one had infinite, never wholly de-fined possibilities. The paper doll is a stand-in for the questing trial-self, for whom as young girls we devised adventurous cos-tumes and outlandish stories of journeys with unknown desti-nations.

In the shtetl myth the pleasures of lawful sex recompense wives for harsh dailiness, the burden of fleshed-out gender, and the ambiguous gift of reproductive power. Somebody's dream, out of an imagined past. As is my flat silhouette doll whose limitless possibilities had no flesh. They are equally pleasant dreams that can become nightmares: The *balabustas* sweeping their corn brooms across the stage turn into witches, wicked stepmothers refusing to nourish the paper girl, fey Petra Pan. Petra, in any case, will not eat because she needs to stay light if she ever wants to fly.

She'd rather come to a bad end, change her name to Icaria.

Or will she settle in, finally, a new Mrs. Shlemiel? Does that possibility exist?

The other play—not necessarily a musical comedy—that begins to suggest itself as the images pull in various directions is being lived now and may already have been written. Domes-tic and sexual, economic, personal, political, multicultural, new/old feminist texts that should run for the next twenty-five years at least, in hundreds of different versions.

ANNE HALLEY, a writer, poet, and translator, wrote the afterwords to *Anna Teller*, a novel by Jo Sinclair (The Feminist Press, 1992) and *The Parish and the Hill*, a novel by Mary Doyle Curran (The Feminist Press, 1986).

Photo by Jules Chametzky.

Voices from Australia

Susan Hawthorne
and Renate Klein

FEMINISM IS THE MOST IMPORTANT POLITICAL MOVEMENT OF THE LATE TWENTIETH CENTURY. FEMINISTS HAVE CHALLENGED EVERYTHING— FROM GROSS VIOLATIONS OF WOMEN ACROSS ALL CULTURES, RACES, CLASSES, RELIGIONS, AND GROUPS— TO THE DEEP AND PERVASIVE CONTROLS OF PATRIARCHAL CAPITALISM. HAVING RETHOUGHT REALITY AND RESEARCHED HISTORY, FEMINISTS HAVE ALSO ATTEMPTED TO IMAGINE OTHER WAYS OF LIVING NOW AND IN THE FUTURE. FEMINISM, LIKE ALL OTHER MOVEMENTS, HAS DRAWN ON PAST POLITICAL SUCCESSES AND THE IDEAS OF OTHER GROUPS (THE LEFT, ANTIRACIST MOVEMENTS, ET CETERA) BUT HAS ALSO EXPOSED THE WEAKNESSES OF SUCH POLITICAL MOVEMENTS, NAMELY THEIR INABILITY TO DEAL WITH "THE PERSONAL IS POLITICAL." THE PERSONAL ELEMENT OF FEMINIST POLITICS HAS ADDED A RICHNESS THAT IS DIFFICULT TO FIND IN OTHER POLITICAL ANALYSES AND IT HAS STRENGTHENED OUR ANALYSIS TO INCLUDE ISSUES AROUND SEXUALITY, DISABILITY, SPIRITUALITY, AND OUR EMOTIONAL LIVES. THIS REFRACTION OF PUBLIC POLITICS WITH PERSONAL POLITICS IS ONE OF THE MOST IMPORTANT INSIGHTS OF FEMINISM TO COME OUT OF THE MOVEMENT DURING THE 1970S, AND IN THAT REGARD NEITHER OF US HAS CHANGED HER OPINION ABOUT ITS CENTRALITY.

Of course, the women's movement has changed since the 1970s—just as we have changed—and the two interact. In our roles as publishers, editors, writers, and academics, we have both contributed to the overall shape of feminist theory and feminist politics—including the development of women's studies—during that period, and in turn have been shaped by changes that have taken place. Twenty-five years ago none of us was aware of the scale of violence against women and the varieties of forms it takes—from medical violence, rape, sexual abuse, and pornography to the more subtle coerciveness of population control policies, consumerism, and control of information resources. We were aware of violence, as many of us had been subjected to it at some stage, but we thought that we were one of the few.

Twenty-five years ago there were no feminist bookshops, art galleries, rock bands. And the few organizations that were beginning to emerge around the world knew nothing of one another's activities. Now there is a plethora of feminist businesses, including hundreds of publishing companies, magazines, women's studies courses, lesbian, black, and indigenous studies courses, and there are electronic bulletin boards where an organization such as UBINIG in Bangladesh can contact another such as FINRRAGE in Australia in seconds, and keep in touch easily and (once you have the hardware, software, and know-how) relatively inexpensively.

Feminist conferences were one of the early "inventions" of the women's movement and have stood us in good stead throughout the period as a means of sharing information, networking, and making important meetings. Feminist conferences have changed many lives—personally and politically—and they continue to do so. But in 1970 we could not have imagined the huge international gatherings that now occur on a regular basis: International Women's Health Conference, the International Feminist Book Fair, the International Interdisciplinary Congress on Women, national women's studies conferences in many countries, and the numerous UN-sponsored conferences, to name just a few.

But to ensure that feminism continues to thrive in the future there are many things we have yet to achieve or consolidate.

We need to subvert the dominant push that the needs of the North and the West are the world's needs. For example, at the September 1994 UN International Conference on Population and Development in Cairo, U.S. women, backed by their government and the Population Council, pushed abortion as the most important issue of the conference. But for women whose countries and sisters are targets of coercive programs, the ability to refuse a forced abortion, sterilization, or unsafe contraceptive methods is as important—no more and no less— as the ability to secure a safe and legal abortion. The ecologically devastating consumerist lifestyle of the North, in particular of the U.S., needs urgent attention. Blaming the poor of the world—and the vast majority of the poor are women and children—will not secure a future for everyone. Consumerism is as important an issue as population.

We need to extend our imaginations, as well as build on our ability to communicate and understand one another. Coming from Australia, we are aware of how little our imaginative work reaches the shores of North America. This is a great loss for those of you from the North. It means you know little about indigenous issues, art, and history in Australia, Aotearoa/New Zealand, and the Pacific (and when you do, it is frequently distorted); you know little about the strength and vitality of our lesbian culture, or of the history of our women's movement (the Cook Islands, Aotearoa/New Zealand and Australia were the earliest countries to give the vote to women). You know little of our visions for the future or of the present conditions of our lives.

One of the reasons we founded Spinifex Press in 1991 was to ensure that the voices of radical feminists from the southern hemisphere, from the Pacific and Asia, and of indigenous women, lesbians, and disabled women would get a hearing internationally. We were also concerned about the way postmodernist feminism had hijacked radical feminist ideas and was assisting in the process of eroding gains and important standpoints. We also believe strongly in the need for an international feminist movement that respects diversity but nevertheless has the ability to respond readily to the many challenges wherever they arise.

SUSAN HAWTHORNE (right) and **RENATE KLEIN** are cofounders of Spinifex Press in North Melbourne, Australia. Authors and editors of many books, they coedited *Australia for Women: Travel and Culture* (The Feminist Press, 1994) which was copublished with Spinifex Press and Frauenoffensive (Germany).

Photo by Renate Sadrozinski.

Re-Visioning Re-Membered

Elaine Hedges

ASKED TO WRITE ABOUT THE FUTURE OF FEMINISM, I BEGIN, AS ONE MUST, BY RE-MEMBERING THE PAST. NINE-TEEN SIXTY-NINE WAS FOR ME ANTI-VIETNAM WAR PLAC-ARDS, PROTESTS AND ARRESTS AT THE MODERN LANGUAGE ASSOCIATION MEETINGS IN NEW YORK AND, AT THOSE SAME HEADY MEETINGS, THE CREATION OF THE MLA COMMISSION ON THE STATUS OF WOMEN, ONE OF THE EARLIEST OF SUCH PROFESSIONAL GROUPS. TWO YEARS LATER I WAS CHAIRING THAT COMMISSION'S SECOND FORUM, WHERE BEFORE AN OVER-FLOW AUDIENCE TILLIE OLSEN PRESENTED "ONE OUT OF TWELVE: WOMEN WHO ARE WRITERS IN OUR CENTURY," LATER TO BECOME THE KEY CHAPTER IN HER BOOK, *SILENCES*; AND ADRIENNE RICH PRESENTED "WHEN WE DEAD AWAKEN: WRITING AS RE-VISION," WHICH ALSO QUICKLY TOOK ITS PLACE AS A CLASSIC OF CONTEMPORARY FEMINISM.

"Re-vision," Rich said in that talk, is "the act of looking back, of seeing with fresh eyes, of entering an old text from a new critical direction." She was referring, of course, to our need to reenter and reread the patriarchal texts of the past, in order to release their hold over us. In the quarter century since then we have done just that, to an extraordinary degree: We have recovered our history, our literature and culture, the record of our past activism, even as in the present we continue to add to that record.

If I here use Rich's words in order to reenter, not the old patriarchal texts, but a few of the feminist texts—now become "old"—that we created a quarter of a century ago, it is because I believe more than ever in the words with which Rich con-cluded her statement: that such acts of reentry and re-vision are for women essential "acts of survival."

My students are often restless when asked to learn his-tory, even their own history as women and as feminists. They want to get on with their own lives, which are more crowded—filled with more demands and distractions—and in many ways more uncertain—will they even find decent jobs?—than ours probably were. In such a context I would ask them to remem-ber (for revisioning is re-membering) one of contemporary feminism's oldest texts—that "the personal is political." It is perhaps more true now than ever, and they neglect it at their peril.

I would ask, too, that they re-member that other old text, lately discredited as sentimental, that "sisterhood is powerful." My students today inherit a feminism in the United States that has become pluralized at best, fractured at worst. In the acad-emy itself they may encounter generational disputes, factional-ism, careerism, competitiveness, and a divorce between academicians and activists. But they may also still find there the nurturing, the bonding, and the sustained effort to build bridges and discover commonalities among the many "feminisms" into which the movement has divided.

I would urge that they think of proliferation rather than division, and proliferation by now, of course, on a global scale. As I write, the third world conference on population planning has just concluded in Cairo, and women's voices, from all races, classes, and regions of the world, were central to that confer-ence as they had not been to previous ones. In September of 1995 over 20,000 women from throughout the world will gather in Beijing, China for the Fourth United Nations Conference on Women. Such meetings, and the activism that both generates them and flows from them, are rooted in forms of sisterhood. Our global diversity demands such sisterhood. Re-membered and re-visioned, the idea of the power of sisterhood is an im-portant part of the legacy of the first generation of the contem-porary feminist movement to those who will carry that movement into the next century.

ELAINE HEDGES is professor of English and director of women's studies at Towson State University. She wrote the afterword to Charlotte Perkins Gilman's *The Yellow Wallpaper* (The Feminist Press, 1973), edited a col-lection of writings by Meridel Le Sueur, *Ripening* (The Feminist Press, 1982), and coedited with Ingrid Wendt *In Her Own Image: Women Working in the Arts* (The Feminist Press, 1980).

Photo by Marietta Hedges.

Nurturance and Commitment

Arlie Russell Hochschild

Without a vision, we wouldn't have taken the first step. To crystalize our vision, we created a movement, and to shelter the movement, we've needed to build institutions. I used to cringe at that inhospitable word, "institution." But if I have learned anything in the last twenty-five years, it is that institutions are the steady keepers of the watch we need so that we feel safe reshaping our visions. Our original vision is still right on. I'd only renew our emphasis on the value of nurturance and commitment as common denominators across all the groups we are. We were taking it for granted before, and we need these more now.

ARLIE RUSSELL HOCHSCHILD is professor of sociology at the University of California, Berkeley. Her books include *The Second Shift: Working Parents and the Revolution at Home*, *The Managed Heart*, and *Coleen the Question Girl* (The Feminist Press, 1974), to be reissued in 1996.

Photo by Eliot Holtzman Photography.

Feminist Sons*

Perdita Huston

I have raised a son alone. His father left when the boy was six weeks old. Over the years I have heard my son grumble even as a small boy to friends about his mother's feminism and how he was made to sit at the dinner table with "all her women friends." When I heard this I wondered if I had done well by him. Had I force-fed him, imposed my thinking on a sensitive growing child?

How difficult it has been, always wondering if I was doing the right thing by exposing my son so totally to my sisterhood commitment, often forgetting that the brotherhood I couldn't offer was also a need in his emerging male world.

My son is now a man of twenty-one, tall, still a bit gangly, and gaining self-confidence in the chaos of university life. He earns his keep by working in a bookstore.

Today he called me from work. Here follows our conversation:

"Mom! Have you seen the latest issue of *Ms.* magazine?"

"It has arrived but I haven't read it yet. Why?"

"It's about fifty ways to be a feminist. There are profiles on fifty feminists and not one of them is a man."

"Are you sure? That would be tragic, sending all the wrong messages …"

"I know. That's what I mean. I think I'll write them to say so. It's demeaning to men who are feminists."

"I'll write, too. I'm disappointed in *Ms.*"

By his call and his comments, my son has made me happy, beyond all I can say here. And he has given us a good lesson. The future of feminism resides in how well we manage the partnership of male and female feminists. Until that partnership becomes the norm, without effort and without restraint, our feminism remains incomplete.

From a letter to the editor of Ms., *August 10, 1994*

PERDITA HUSTON, a journalist living in Washington, D.C., is the author of *Motherhood by Choice: Pioneers in Women's Health and Family Planning* (The Feminist Press, 1992).

Photo by Jerry Bauer.

Two Become One

Hadley Irwin

ONLY AN INSTANT AGO—WELL, IN 1979—THE FEMINIST PRESS GAVE BIRTH TO A WRITER CALLED HADLEY IRWIN. OF COURSE, SHE WAS NEARLY ONE HUNDRED YEARS OLD AT THE TIME AND HADN'T BEEN PUBLISHED BEFORE AND NOBODY AT THE PRESS KNEW IF SHE WAS MALE OR FEMALE BUT THEY WERE WILLING TO READ HER FIRST BOOK, *THE LILITH SUMMER*. EVEN MORE WONDERFUL, THE PRESS PUBLISHED IT AND KEPT ALIVE A WOMAN (TWO) WHO, LIKE THAT DAMN PINK BUNNY, JUST KEPT ON GOING AND…WELL, NEVER MIND.

How was the world for women then? Well, even though we sent a manuscript to The Press, we chose Hadley Irwin as our name. Not Annabelle Lee. Certainly not Irwin Hadley. Why? Someone else had first dibs on the former. The latter sounded pot-bellied, male, and bald. Were we sexist, or what?

More important than the name was the book we sent. It was about the child we might have been, about the woman we would like to become. It was about life and love, about beauty and death and the eternal strength of woman. Not women. Woman. The Feminist Press published the book. We still receive letters from readers who feel Lilith's presence.

And then, *We Are Mesquakie, We Are One*. A big chance for The Press; a big chance for us. We are not Mesquakie and we could have done something untrue, no matter what our best intents. But two women, Gretchen Bataille and Adalaine Wanatee, cared enough to read the manuscript before publication and, because of their belief and their knowledge, assured us that the book spoke as it should. And The Press agreed.

Both of those books were about women; both of them were written by a woman. Well, by two women who grew from writing what we felt could be to what we know is certain: We are women; we are one. We are also as varied as the seeds blown by the wind.

What differences! What beauty! At the age of one hundred thirty-nine, Hadley Irwin is still re-visioning and reliving feminism. Take it from us—words can change the world. It just takes time. Twenty-five years is a wonderful start.

HADLEY IRWIN is the pen name of LEE HADLEY (right) and ANNABELLE IRWIN, native Iowans, who teach English at Iowa State University, Ames. Together they wrote *The Lilith Summer* (The Feminist Press, 1979) and *We Are Mesquakie, We Are One* (The Feminist Press, 1980).

Achievements and Mistakes

Rounaq Jahan

I SUPPOSE I WAS A FEMINIST ALL MY LIFE EVEN BEFORE THE TERM WAS COINED AND BECAME FASHIONABLE IN THE LATE 1960S. AS I WAS GROWING UP IT WAS DIFFICULT NOT TO BE ACUTELY AWARE OF THE INJUSTICES OF THE SOCIALLY-IMPOSED LIMITS ON MY CHOICES, MOBILITY, AND ASPIRATIONS. FREEDOM TO CHOOSE MY OWN DESTINY, TO BE KNOWN AND APPRECIATED IN MY OWN NAME—NOT AS THE DAUGHTER, WIFE, OR MOTHER OF SOMEBODY—WAS ALL I WANTED. I WAS, HOWEVER, NOT A REBEL. I KNEW FROM MY CHILDHOOD THAT, TO BE ABLE TO SET MY OWN AGENDA, I WOULD HAVE TO GAIN ECONOMIC INDEPENDENCE, AND THE ONLY WAY TO ACCOMPLISH THAT, IN MY CIRCUMSTANCES, WAS THROUGH ACHIEVEMENT IN EDUCATION. GETTING OUTSTANDING GRADES IN SCHOOLS AND WINNING SCHOLARSHIPS APPEARED TO BE THE ONLY THINGS WITHIN MY CONTROL, AND SO I CHOSE THAT ROUTE TO CLAIM MY IDENTITY AND VOICE.

No doubt the strategies I chose in my personal life influenced the strategies I pursued in advocating the cause of gender equality. In Bangladesh, I tended to be cautious, always hedging against negative fallout, always striving to move the cause forward without direct confrontation. As I look back on my own experiences of advocacy during the past two decades, I realize that I did play an important role, I did succeed in many ways. But I also realize I made some major mistakes. What are the things I remember with pride? What are the mistakes I now regret?

I remember with pride how a few of us in the early 1970s struggled and bonded across countries and regions to make the women's movement international. I remember vividly Bucharest '74, Mexico '75, Wellesley '76, Tehran '77, Stony Brook '79, and Copenhagen '80. We—women from North and South—differed and clashed but out of the confrontation and dialogue developed an understanding of each other's priorities and positions. I also remember Nairobi '85, when we all came together united in our common goals and respecting our differences.

I remember the excitement of the 1970s when a few of us were struggling to make gender issues a concern of policymakers and development planners in Bangladesh. The women's movement had always been there in the country. But for the first time we took up the challenge of lobbying the economic policymakers and planners. I particularly remember how my hopes were raised when, in his speech inaugurating the first South and Southeast Asian Conference on Women and Development held in Dhaka in 1977 (I organized the conference as well as wrote the president's speech), our head of government for the first time made a strong public policy commitment on gender equality.

Of course, in hindsight it is easy now to recognize my mistakes. I think I made a mistake in devoting so much of my energy in lobbying policymakers through demonstrations of evidence and data. I now feel I focused too much on getting all the technical arguments right. Instead I should have spent a lot more of my time and energy in enhancing the mass base of the women's movement. Ideas and writings can sow the seeds, but major social change comes about only when a sufficiently large number of people are mobilized in favor of change. I have devoted my energies to the realm of ideas and writings but left others to do the mobilization work.

My other mistake, I feel, was my intellectual arrogance. In the 1970s when I was trying to influence policy changes in Bangladesh, I often acted very much alone. That limited the results. For example, I was able to get a policy commitment by writing the president's speech in 1977, but there was very little follow up, as I did not have with me a group to build continuous pressure on the government to deliver on its promises.

During the last two decades, the women's movement in Bangladesh has certainly gained strength. Its mass base is still narrow but there is much greater public awareness. I remember in 1973 a colleague joking that there was only one publicly-acknowledged feminist in Bangladesh! These days I meet many young Bengali *men* who openly acknowledge that *they* are feminists! "Feminism" and "feminist" are by now familiar and frequently used terms in the Bengali language—one does not have to use the English term: another sign of change and progress.

Certainly I find a difference between our generation and the present generation of feminists. As I meet the young generation, I realize how I must have come across to my older generation in Bangladesh. I now have a much greater sense of the women's movement as a long historical process. I now appreciate much more what the previous generation of activists did—whether they called themselves feminists or not. I know that I played a part in my own time as others did before me and as others will after me.

ROUNAQ JAHAN, adjunct professor of international affairs at Columbia University, is author of *The Elusive Agenda: Mainstreaming Women in Development* and an afterword to *Seeds 2: Supporting Women's Work* (The Feminist Press, 1995).

The Statement of a Sibyl

Elizabeth Janeway

IF I AM ALIVE TO CHECK THE VALIDITY OF THIS PREDICTION IN TWENTY-FIVE YEARS, I WILL BE ONE HUNDRED AND SIX YEARS OLD, SO PLEASE TREAT MY WORDS AS THE STATEMENT OF A SIBYL. IF I AM NOT, WE CAN ALL FORGET ABOUT IT. TO BE SERIOUS—I BELIEVE THAT FEMINISM WILL CERTAINLY BE ALIVE, WELL, AND FORCEFULLY ACTIVE. WE WILL NOT HAVE FULL EQUALITY, I EXPECT. THAT ENDEAVOR COULD REQUIRE CENTURIES, BUT WE ARE ON THE WAY. AND ALONG THE WAY, LET ME REMIND YOU THAT EQUALITY DOES NOT MEAN SAMENESS. WHAT IT DOES MEAN, IN A MONEY ECONOMY, IS AN OPPORTUNITY FOR ALL TO EARN WHATEVER THAT PERSON NEEDS THROUGH ANY CHOSEN JOB OR PROFESSION. STILL, TALENT AND DRIVE ARE NOT SET BY SEXUAL LIMITS.

The problem that human families still face is the traditional expectation that their first job is in the home. Well, not too long ago, a large percentage of people earned a living at home—because homes and workshops shared the same space. Farmers lived on farms; spinning wheels and looms occupied living areas; blacksmiths lived next door to their forges; and skilled craftsmen and their apprentices worked and lived in rooms attached to or next to their work space. Their children might well grow up into their fathers' trades or occupations. Women, young and old, were very much a part of home manufacture.

When paid work moved out of the home, a lot of unpaid work stayed behind. Raising a family was a vital, central part of it. The house and the children turned into women's work, and in the main, housework and child raising still occupy the same dimension. Redefining this status isn't impossible, but it still has not happened in a major fashion. The practical solution of child care centers at places of work came up twenty years ago, but they were not established to any considerable degree in the U.S. and seem to have been largely dismissed as expensive, destructive to "family values," and therefore avoidable. The result: Most working women can't both earn a decent living and undertake the family work and presence that creates a solid background for growing up. I regard serious attention to this social and psychological question as vital—and entirely possible. Marriage and economics—you can't have one without the other.

ELIZABETH JANEWAY, novelist and social critic, is author of five novels, including *Leaving Home* (The Feminist Press, 1987).

Girls Who Love Dogs

Bobbi Katz

WHEN I FIRST WROTE THE STORY OF MY DAUGHTER'S LONGING FOR A DOG AND STARTED SENDING IT TO CHILDREN'S PUBLISHERS, THE RESPONSES WERE MIXED. EDITORS SUGGESTED THAT THERE WAS SOMETHING "NOT QUITE NORMAL" ABOUT A LITTLE GIRL WANTING A DOG SO MUCH. MAYBE I COULD "RETHINK" THE STORY WITH A BOY AS THE MAIN CHARACTER OR "TRY KEEPING THE GIRL AND MAKE THE DOG A HORSE." THERE WAS SOMETHING ABOUT THIS TREE-CLIMBING-FISH-CATCHING-TRUMPET-PLAYING-ICE-SKATING KID—THIS ACTIVE GIRL—THAT MADE THE LADIES WITH THE RED PENS UNCOMFORTABLE.

Luckily, I heard about The Feminist Press from Esther Gilman, whom I met at a class in writing and illustrating children's books at the New School. And The Feminist Press liked my manuscript. Esther spent a couple of days sketching my "not quite normal" daughter, and I provided her with a bunch of snapshots of Lori doing all the things she usually did. Before long, *Nothing But a Dog* was published and received glowing reviews.

Inspired by my daughter and The Feminist Press, I went on to publish chapter books about active girls and two first-person books about girl activists. (Both of them were banned in West Virginia and Texas.) Several years later I moved to New York and became an editor at a mass-market publishing house. A big part of my job was actually writing book after book featuring licenced characters. No royalties were added to my salary, but I had a wonderful opportunity to create stories with can-do female characters, even if they were pastel-colored bears who slide down rainbows. Every once in a while, I had an easy job when a license like the Handy Girls came along.

By the 1980s all the copy editors I knew were hip to non-sexist language. And as The Feminist Press celebrates twenty-five years, feisty girls abound in books for young readers. Active girls are even well established in typical "boys" books like the Young Indiana Jones stories. Whenever a girl is involved, she's every bit as brave and as smart as young Indy himself.

I recently left my job to write full-time and to play the drums. I've been busy with some practical projects to pay the rent, including a biography of Nelson Mandela for kids (that unexpectedly turned into an obsessive passion). Now I want to focus on creating collections of my poems.

Regardless of what kind of girl will speak in my poems and my stories, I know there will be no problems with editors changing her sex. Thanks to The Feminist Press, it's now okay to write about girls who love dogs more than horses and prefer using tools to playing with Barbie dolls.

P. S. My "not quite normal" daughter managed to grow up and has her own business, Eco-Explorations; she teaches scuba diving, sea kayaking, and underwater photography, and leads trips to fabulous places for adventurous women.

BOBBI KATZ, a former editor at Random House, is a children's author, poet, and biographer. She has written several collections of poetry, children's books—including *Nothing But a Dog* (The Feminist Press, 1972)—and environmental essays.

To Reach Deeper

Montana Katz

IN THE PAST TWENTY-FIVE YEARS, MUCH HAS HAPPENED IN THE WORLD THAT FEMINISTS CAN CELEBRATE. A GOOD DEAL OF THE CHANGE, HOWEVER, HAS BEEN SURFACE LEVEL. IN THE TWENTY-FIVE YEARS TO COME, I HOPE THAT WE CAN REACH DEEPER. ONE WAY THAT THIS COULD HAPPEN IS BY APPROXIMATING ENVIRONMENTS FREE FROM GENDER STEREOTYPES FOR OUR CHILDREN FROM BIRTH ON. WITH SUCH AN INTRODUCTION TO THE WORLD, GIRLS WOULD READILY SEE THE DIFFERENCE IN THE LARGER COMMUNITY. THEY WOULD GROW IN CONTRAST TO THEIR MOTHERS WHO, AS ADULTS, EACH HAD TO REINVENT THE WHEEL IN VIRTUAL SOLITUDE TO GAIN THAT SAME RECOGNITION. THESE GIRLS WOULD KNOW THAT ALL THE PROBLEMS FACING WOMEN HAVE NOT BEEN SOLVED AND WOULD BE BETTER EQUIPPED THAN THEIR FOREMOTHERS TO EFFECT LASTING CHANGE.

MONTANA KATZ is in residence at the Barnard College Center for Research on Women and is a post-doctoral scholar in cognitive psychology at Columbia University. She is coauthor with Veronica Vieland of *Get Smart! What You Should Know (But Won't Learn in Class) About Sexual Harassment and Sex Discrimination*, Second Edition (The Feminist Press, 1993), which won a 1994 Outstanding Book Citation from the Gustavus Myers Center for the Study of Human Rights in North America.

Community and Power

Martha Kearns

I WAS HISTORICALLY LUCKY, COMING OF AGE IN THE UNITED STATES IN THE LATE SIXTIES, TO BE PART OF ONE PASSIONATE SOCIAL AND PO-LITICAL REVOLUTIONARY MOVEMENT AFTER ANOTHER, FROM CIVIL RIGHTS AND THE VIETNAM ANTIWAR MOVE-MENT TO THE WOMEN'S MOVEMENT. WITH EACH OF THESE CAME FIRE IN THE BLOOD, IN MINE, IN THOUSANDS, FOR SOCIAL, POLITICAL, AND ECONOMIC JUSTICE, FOR THE INFINITELY DIFFICULT YET HOPEFUL CONDITION OF PEACE.

I believe there are two realities from then which we need to remember and use as we create our world beyond the millenium. I believe feminism contributed new definitions, in idea and practice, to community and power.

In spirit and behavior the community was generous toward the abilities and circumstances of individuals. These were sincere encouragement, the practice of respectful listening, and active political, social, or economic help by women to women of class or ethnic backgrounds different from theirs. This spirit of generosity changed for the better the lives of thousands of women, perhaps millions now, here in the United States. It also added, by practice, the idea of individuality to the meaning of community.

The Western notion of power, deriving, for the most part, on physical might and/or military strength, opposes the femi-nist. The feminist concept, in principle and practice, is *in situ;* it is contextual, relational, associative. Its authority comes from the experience a woman has of the ability to sustain human life, and is ethical.

The obstacle to feminist power has been and will be, on a social level, fear of the loss of strength or control by men over women, and, on the political and economic level, war.

Is it possible we humans can live without war?

We humans can sustain life.

Will we?

As we create a human future, the realities of feminist community and feminist power are a necessity.

MARTHA KEARNS is an art historian, critic, and author of *Käthe Kollwitz: Woman and Artist* (The Feminist Press 1976).

Photo by Wayne Cozzolino.

A Shifting Mosaic

Alice Kessler-Harris

IN 1970, WHEN THE FEMI-NIST PRESS WAS FOUNDED, FEMINISM WAS AN EXCITING WORD—IT CAPTURED SUCH A VAST RANGE OF POSSIBILITIES FOR HUMAN FREEDOM THAT ITS CAPACITIES TO REFIGURE ITSELF SEEMED UNLIMITED. TWENTY-FIVE YEARS LATER, FEMINISM REMAINS AN EXPLOSIVE, EVEN REVOLUTIONARY, IDEA WHOSE POWER WE CAN GAUGE BY THE ANGER IT STILL MUSTERS AMONG THOSE WHO FEAR IT. I HAVE BEEN CAUGHT UP OVER THESE PAST YEARS IN THE TRANSFORMATIVE POWER OF THE WORD AND WHAT IT REPRESENTS. BECAUSE FEMINISM ENCOMPASSES THE DESIRE FOR HUMAN EQUALITY AND KEEPS ITS IMAGE ALIVE IN A WORLD WHERE CYNICISM IS RIFE, IT HOLDS THE POSSIBILITY FOR POSITIVE SOCIAL CHANGE. BECAUSE FEMINISM IS KALEIDOSCOPIC, IT CAN AND DOES RESHAPE ITSELF SO THAT IT IS LESS A BLUEPRINT THAN A SHIFTING MOSAIC THROUGH WHICH WE MAKE SENSE OF THE WORLD AROUND US. BECAUSE FEMINISM RE-VISIONS ITSELF CONSTANTLY, IT RELENTLESSLY INSISTS THAT EACH OF US CONTINUALLY INTERROGATES THE NOTIONS OF WOMAN-HOOD THAT PROVIDE THE SOURCE OF A COMMON "WE." THE CURRENT RE-VISIONING OF U.S. FEMINISM, WHICH SEEKS TO UNDERSTAND THE MEANING OF THE GROUND ON WHICH WE STAND FROM A LESS LOCAL AND A MORE GLOBAL PERSPECTIVE, HOLDS ENORMOUS PROMISE. AS I THINK ABOUT HOW MANY FORMS OF HUMAN FREEDOM ARE ENCOMPASSED BY THE NO-TION OF FEMINISM, I AM STRUCK AT HOW COMFORTABLY THE FEMINIST PRESS MANAGES TO SPEAK TO THEM ALL—LEADING THE WAY, MARKING THE PATH, PROVIDING THE SUPPORTING MATERIALS THAT ENABLE US ALL TO MOVE FORWARD.

ALICE KESSLER-HARRIS is professor of history and director of women's studies at Rutgers University, New Brunswick. She is the author of *Women Have Always Worked: An Historical Overview* (The Feminist Press, 1981).

Photo by Andrew Kessler.

Ms. Nomers

Edith Konecky

I HAVE ALWAYS DISLIKED THE WORD "FEMINISM," NOT FOR WHAT IT STANDS FOR BUT FOR WHAT IT IMPLIES. THERE IS NO SUCH WORD AS "MASCULISM" BECAUSE THERE HAS BEEN NO NEED FOR IT. IT MAKES MY BLOOD BOIL THAT THERE WAS AND STILL IS A NEED FOR THE WORD "FEMINISM," WHICH, IN THE CONTEXT OF GENDER, MEANS NOT SAMENESS BUT POLITICAL, SOCIAL, AND ECONOMIC EQUALITY.

When I was in my teens my family bought a house in Briarcliff Manor that had belonged to Carrie Chapman Catt, who had died not long before. She had been, I knew, a "suffragette," another dreadful word that brought to mind a row of women in bloomers kicking up their heels, like the Rockettes. I really hadn't given it much thought, but when we moved into her house, a wonderful house filled with peace and a balm-like light and stillness, it was difficult to believe that it must still hold some trace of the spirit of its former owner. A "suffragette," my dictionary said, is a woman who *militantly* (emphasis mine) advocated the right of women to vote. Ancient history, I'd thought, but it wasn't ancient history, it was very recent history, and my blood boiled then, too. Unimaginable that it should have been commonly and universally accepted, even by many women, that women not have the right to vote. Unimaginable that there has always been, in one degree or another, usefulness for the word "feminism." In optimistic moments I tell myself that soon, at least in this part of the world, both words will be equally archaic.

EDITH KONECKY is a writer whose books include *A Place at the Table* and *Allegra Maud Goldman* (The Feminist Press, 1990).

Photo by Joanna Eldredge Morrissey.

Am I the Doomsayer?

Susan Koppelman

I HAVE BEEN ASKED TO WRITE SOMETHING ABOUT WHAT I THINK WILL BE THE FUTURE OF FEMINISM. I HAVE BEEN ASKED TO DO THIS IN ORDER TO PARTICIPATE IN THE CELEBRATION OF THE TWENTY-FIFTH YEAR OF THE SURVIVAL OF THE FEMINIST PRESS, A VENTURE I HAVE WATCHED SINCE THE VERY BEGINNING. BUT WHAT IF I HAVE ONLY PESSIMISM TO SHARE? IS THAT A WAY TO PARTICIPATE IN A CELEBRATION? TO BE THE DOOMSAYER AT A BIRTHDAY PARTY…

So I will say this: If I could not be optimistic about our future—as feminists, as human beings, as lovers and friends and parents and artists and workers, as a species—on this planet or elsewhere as the case may be (just so it isn't nowhere, because that's not optimistic) and as citizens of a planet that might do better without us, I could not continue. I manage to continue. So far.

Maybe we'll be all right. If we get the conversations between and among the generations right this time. If we remember to include all of our various selves in our great variety of manifestations and all of our selves assume our rights to be included. If we do it our way and not Frank's or Sammy's.

SUSAN KOPPELMAN is editor of eight anthologies, including *The Other Woman: Stories of Two Women and a Man* (The Feminist Press, 1984) and *Between Mothers and Daughters: Stories across a Generation* (The Feminist Press, 1985).

Beyond National Egotism

*Gerlinde Kowitzke
and Hilke Schlaeger*

Times when radical feminists and Nazis are publicly named in one breath cannot be good times. The feminist purpose—changing society to create a place where women (and men and children) can live their lives in human decency in an atmosphere of non-violence and social justice—has been pushed back to the margins of the socially unimaginable in these times when utopian aspirations are regarded as suspicious, and the happiness of the individual features as the most radical of all possible visions. We see more than the collapse of socialist states and the ensuing discrediting of the dream of justice and equality. We see the brutalization of various societies around the world, especially these last five years. The balance of powers, kept in an equilibrium throughout all of the hot and cold wars, is lost; what we have is the unbalance of terror.

That this world has limits, that resources do not last forever, that the earth cannot provide for the people wanting to live on its face if people continue working to destroy it, is understood mainly by women, for they are the first to suffer. Suffering makes you smart—and practical. Thus the feminist project remains the most modern of all projects for the world of tomorrow. International feminism still presents the avant-garde of political philosophy. If we did not believe in it, we would assimilate into a system that calls prudent what has immediate results in dollars and cents, that calls successful what does away with competition most effectively, and that calls realistic what shams best. We would confirm what we have been fighting against all the time: that there must always be rulers and subjects, winners and losers, exploiters and exploited (plus all those that flee responsibility by "constructing" and "deconstructing" in the refined postmodern mode). We would not only betray feminism, but the future, in a very practical sense.

So, what do we need? Feminists in the year 1995 do not have to reinvent the wheel. What we have to do instead is remember what got the new women's movement going twenty-five years ago. Its strength was its consciousness of the community among women regardless of their individual differences and a sense of international solidarity beyond any national egotism. We have made a number of mistakes since—not all of us have done everything wrong, but we have all made enough mistakes to despair now and then. Some of us have given up the feminist project for a more or less comfortable seat at the table of the establishment. Others have gone through the most painful contortions to stay feminist on the one hand, while on the other striving to be accepted as the "good girl" once more. Some have worn themselves out in sisterliness and have not been able to bear the lack of love. But some—albeit in conflict and sometimes in exaggeration—have gone on developing the ideas of community and solidarity: black women, white women, Jewish women, lesbians. We know more today, and we know more about each other.

In times when radical feminists are called right-wing fundamentalists, it cannot suffice to preserve what we have, for that will not stop it being taken away. What we must do is take a fresh start, and be smarter this time.

GERLINDE KOWITZKE (right) and HILKE SCHLAEGER are cofounders and directors of the German feminist press Frauenoffensive, original publishers of Verena Stefan's *Shedding* (The Feminist Press, 1994) and founders of the Travel for Women series which includes *Australia for Women* (The Feminist Press, 1994) and *China for Women* (The Feminist Press, 1995).

Strong and Capable

K. Lalita

IT IS NOT POSSIBLE TO TALK ABOUT A SINGLE TYPE OF FEMINISM OR HOMOGENOUS WOMEN'S MOVEMENT ANYMORE IN ANY PART OF THE WORLD. THIS AWARENESS IS GROWING DUE TO THE ARTICULATION OF THE GENDER QUESTION IN *DALIT* AND MINORITY COMMUNITIES IN INDIA.

A decade ago I thought differently about women and men. My view was, women are always at the receiving end—oppressed and exploited. No longer do I think in these terms. I see women as strong and capable—not just managing their own lives but the world around them. Of course in the process they are being burdened with enormous responsibilities.

Similarly, there is a shift in my perception of men. They no longer appear "all-powerful." It is an amazing revelation for me that men are actually weak and sometimes dependent. That is probably the reason why society needs to keep alive the ideologies that continue to project men as strong.

In any case, I must say I live in a turbulent and exciting period as a great deal is happening everywhere.

Glad You Were There

Susie Tharu

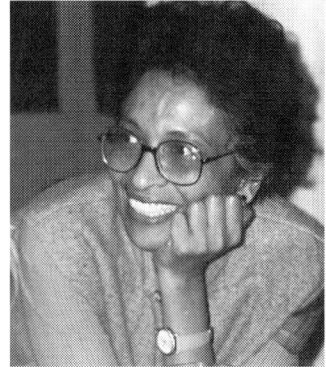

THANK YOU FOR BEING ENGAGED ENOUGH TO TEACH AND WISE ENOUGH TO LEARN. WE ARE GLAD YOU WERE THERE, FEMINIST PRESS, FOR *WOMEN WRITING IN INDIA*.

K. LALITA is a political scientist and coordinator of Anveshi Research Centre for Women's Studies at Osmania University in Hyderabad, India. SUSIE THARU teaches in the English literature department at the Central Institute of English and Foreign Languages in Hyderbad, India. They are coeditors of *Women Writing in India: 600 B.C. to the Early Twentieth Century* (The Feminist Press, 1991) and *Women Writing in India: The Twentieth Century* (The Feminist Press, 1993).

Of Fortresses and Feminists

Tobe Levin

AT 11:45 ON OPENING DAY—THE MEETING WAS STARTING AT 12:00—I ASKED THE TAXI TO PLEASE RUSH ME TO THE BAYEN TOWER. "OH," THE DRIVER, WITH A COMPLICITOUS SMILE, REPLIED, "YOU MEAN THE WOMAN TOWER?"

I had been thinking of a line from Susan Neiman's *Slow Fire*—"So what's it like to grow up in a country without castles?"—as I entered the egg-shell Mercedes in Cologne and named my destination, a fortress erected between 1180 and 1250, paid for not by the feudal lords of the time, but by the class in emergence, the bourgeoisie. Today the monument, rebuilt from semi-ruins, would be dedicated to another class with waxing power, feminists: We would soon be saying "Cheers!" to the FrauenMediaTurm, a major archive for the contemporary German women's movement. "But please don't think of us as a mere repository," founder Alice Schwarzer cautioned her governing board. "We don't want simply to react, record, recollect. We want to shape events, be a motor for the movement." As Ursula Scheu, cochair of the project, flashed a smile at me, I was inaudibly applauding. "Bravo!" my mind bounced: The activist and the academic meet.

Having eagerly looked forward to this August 26, 1994, I wasn't disappointed. Politicians and professors had answered Schwartzer's call. Anke Brunn, Minister of Education in the state of North-Rhine Westphalia; Dorothee Vorbeck, a member emerita of the Hesse government; and Heide Pfarr, previously minister in Berlin and Hesse, joined professors Metz-Göckel, Möhrmann, Neusel, Reinhold, Reiger, and me to admire the architect's blending of modern and medieval while discussing the future of German women's studies. The board's collective influence reveals the astonishing strides of a movement that has traditionally been far more isolated from the "average woman" than American feminism has been. They say that in the U.S. you often hear, "Although I'm a feminist, I disagree [with this or that]." In Germany, it's the opposite: "I'm not a feminist but…" Things are changing, slowly.

And later, over a Pils in the cobbled courtyard a stone's throw from the Rhein, Sigrid Metz-Göckel, head of sociology in Dortmund, will tell me about her graduate students' projects: Half a dozen have chosen Jewish themes, so will I come give a talk? she asks. In Dortmund, they have no Jewish women colleagues. Of course, I nod. My pleasure. My real, if somewhat ironic, ambivalent pleasure. Although we don't articulate the reason why Dortmund has no Jews, an emotional seismograph would capture our shared embarrassment. Not of professorial rank myself, I've been asked to join this gathering in recognition of my international connections: As a cofounder of WISE (Women's International Studies Europe), the association's newsletter editor, and a multilingual feminist, I could of course be of use in advising an archive. But it helps that I'm American by birth, and Jewish. I'm tempted to explain that the hundreds of thousands of Germans you saw on TV parading through the city streets with candles in the fall of 1992 are the real ones, people of good will who include more than your average share of philosemites. It seems an appropriate moment to admit that my current inclusion in a group of German feminist leaders fits with my experience going back to emigration. Why am I still here, so many years after 1975? In large part because one German feminist after another opened her arms in welcome. (In particular, Dagmar, Susanna, Gaby, Angelika, I'm thinking of you.) And over the years, Christian or secular white activists have been learning to treasure the perspectives minority populations have to offer. Afro-German, Turkish, and Spanish women writers publishing in German have begun to find an audience. Of course, other Jewish women will tell you other stories: but mine is positive and offers at least one example of harmonious striving towards a common goal.

TOBE LEVIN teaches U.S. minority women's literature and women's Holocaust memoirs at the University of Maryland, European Division and J.W. Goethe University in Frankfurt, Germany. She wrote the afterword to Verena Stefan's *Shedding & Literally Dreaming* (The Feminist Press, 1994).

Photo by Tobe Levin.

Feminism at the End of the Twentieth Century

Ralph E. Luker

AT THE END OF THE TWENTIETH CENTURY, FEMINISM IS BOTH MORE DEEPLY ROOTED IN AMERICAN CULTURE AND LESS DEEPLY DIVIDED THAN IT WAS AT THE END OF THE NINETEENTH CENTURY. THE CURRENT SITUATION CONTRASTS STARKLY WITH THAT OF AMERICAN FEMINISM AT THAT TIME. THEN, VIRTUALLY ALL OF ITS LEADING ADVOCATES WERE, BY REASON OF THEIR ADVOCACY, CONSIDERED RADICAL CRITICS OF THEIR SOCIETY. EVEN SO, THESE FEMINIST CRITICS OF LATE NINETEENTH-CENTURY AMERICAN CULTURE WERE THEMSELVES SEVERELY DIVIDED BY ISSUES OF CLASS, ETHNICITY, AND IDEOLOGY THAT ARE RECOGNIZABLE, BUT MORE MUTED AND SUBTLE, IN CONTEMPORARY FEMINIST DISCUSSIONS.

Current discussions between communitarian and individualistic versions of feminism were anticipated in the late nineteenth century by Charlotte Perkins Gilman's communal vision, as contrasted, for example, with Elizabeth Cady Stanton's individualistic conception of feminism. Single-issue politics occasionally threatens to divide late twentieth-century feminism; often, it motivates some of feminism's most extreme and dangerous opponents.

Emma Goldman sought to transcend individual differences by grounding a feminist appeal for universal liberation in the class struggle. Yet, her anarchist feminist vision largely alienated Goldman's followers from mainstream American feminism's demand for the franchise. That was single-issue politics at its worst, she thought. What value was there in participating in a fundamentally oppressive system, which co-opted the liberation struggle by enfranchising the oppressed? Goldman's anarchist feminism included the demand for contraceptive rights, but from her point of view Margaret Sanger's crusade for those rights was also single-issue politics. Single-minded emphasis on the franchise or on contraceptive rights, she believed, betrayed the mentality of a middle-class reformer who largely ignored the plight of working-class men and women.

Ida B. Wells's anti-lynching crusade may have seemed to be single-issue politics to many white feminist contemporaries, but it addressed fundamental rights to life and due legal process. The issue was clouded by accusations that lynching's victims were commonly guilty of molesting white women and children. Although Wells disputed the accusation, the indifference of temperance crusader Frances Willard, suffragette Anna Howard Shaw, and many Southern white feminists to the rights of African Americans appalled her. There was tension, however, even in Wells's relationships with white feminists who supported her cause. There was a sense of personal slight from Mary White Ovington, the certainty that Jane Addams too readily accepted the usual excuse for lynching, and the recognition with Susan B. Anthony that, while they supported each other's causes, they had different priorities. It all fed Wells's sense that white feminists were more committed to white women than to racial justice.

The deep roots of late twentieth-century American feminism in the culture are signaled by the development of feminist groups in apparently unlikely places and around unlikely ideological positions, such as evangelical feminists or Feminists for Life. Such groups point to the remarkable maturation in American feminism. Given such depth, an American feminism for the twenty-first century, remembering the witness of Emma Goldman and Ida B. Wells, will insist upon the necessity of solidarity across ancient lines of race and social class.

RALPH E. LUKER is author of *The Social Gospel in Black and White: American Racial Reform, 1885-1912* and coeditor of Volumes I and II of *The Papers of Martin Luther King, Jr.* for which he was nominated for a Pulitzer Prize. He is editor of *Black and White Sat Down Together: The Reminiscences of an NAACP Founder* by Mary White Ovington (The Feminist Press, 1995).

Photo by Dennie Eagleson.

What I Want for Feminism

Jane Marcus

NOW REALLY IS THE TIME FOR ALL GOOD WOMEN TO COME TO THE AID OF ALL OUR VARIOUS FEMINISMS, IN THE STREETS, IN THE PROTECTION OF OUR HARD-WON RIGHT TO ABORTION, IN THE UNIVERSITIES, IN CAMPAIGNS FOR MEDICAL CARE AND AIDS RESEARCH, IN LOCAL AND NATIONAL POLITICS, IN INTERNATIONAL MOVEMENTS FOR EDUCATION AND HEALTH CARE FOR WOMEN AND CHILDREN, FOR GAY AND LESBIAN RIGHTS, FOR RACIAL EQUITY AND REAL ETHNIC REPRESENTATION AT EVERY LEVEL IN THE INSTITUTIONS THAT AFFECT OUR LIVES.

As a mother I want to see the new generations provided for materially and nurtured in feminist ethics. As a feminist activist I want to see our basic rights as women protected fiercely from the murderous onslaught of the rabid Right. As a white middle-class intellectual born in the working class, I want to see black, Hispanic, and new immigrant communities of women given the same opportunities that I was given.

As a feminist critic I want to learn to stop being defensive. As a feminist teacher I want to keep learning from my students. My own agenda is to retreat from the public world of building women's studies programs. As a feminist scholar I want to encourage work on race and gender in myself, my students, and my colleagues. The changes we have brought about in the disciplines are marvelous, and they must be cherished and preserved and handed on to the next generations. As a woman writer, I hope to find my voice and write. And, most of all, I want to see us break this deadly American silence about class.

JANE MARCUS is Distinguished Professor of English at City College and the Graduate Center, CUNY. She wrote the introduction to *The Convert* by Elizabeth Robins (The Feminist Press, 1980), and the afterwords to *Sister Gin* by June Arnold (The Feminist Press, 1989), *Not So Quiet...* by Helen Zenna Smith (The Feminist Press, 1989), and *We That Were Young* by Irene Rathbone (The Feminist Press, 1989).

Photo by Midge McKenzie.

The Future of International Feminism

Vina Mazumdar

Feminism's future, in my view, rests with increasing solidarity of the international women's movement and its ability to transcend the political, cultural, economic, and religious divides that characterize today's global scene. The dreams of "one world" and shared universal values provided the backdrop for the United Nations and the Universal Declaration of Human Rights. Decolonization and the subsequent expansion of membership of the United Nations created both a climate and a series of new opportunities for nations across the world to participate in debates to hammer out common strategies and goals for the future of humanity. The feminist dreams also received a fresh impetus from this backdrop of hope that the future would be different for women the world over than it had been in the past.

The fiftieth anniversary of the United Nations is going to be celebrated when its survival and credibility are being doubted by an increasing number of people across the world. The end of the cold war, instead of making the future more secure, has widened the arenas of armed conflict and traffic in arms, drugs, and human beings, of which women and children are the major victims. As the *Human Development Report 1994* sums up, globalization of prosperity and poverty has increased inequality, the "weakening of social fabrics," rising violence and crime, and the extension of threats to human security "which respect no national borders."

During the seventies and eighties the international women's movement and feminism made substantial advances in bringing women from different corners of the world closer to each other, as they learned to share and respect each other's priorities and perspectives on issues of development, culture, and the specificity of sociopolitical systems. Many of us boasted on different platforms that the women's movement was able to achieve far greater genuine international cooperation and collaboration than our governments. Some of the best examples of these meetings have occurred in very recent years: the Miami World Conference on Women for a Healthier Planet and the Women's Tribunal preceding the World Conference on Human Rights.

As we struggled to understand each other's problems through dialogues and collaboration in research, at conferences, and in the search for alternative strategies to expand women's effective voices in decisions governing national or global affairs, we also discovered that struggles against global inequalities and exploitation needed similar struggle within our own countries, societies, and cultures. We discovered that the conflict was not only between the North and the South in terms of geography and culture, but that there was a south in the North and a north in the South. This, more than anything else, brought the women and development debate center stage, giving a new purpose and sense of direction to women's studies—forcing each of us to look at the diversities within our own countries, finding parallels in women's history elsewhere, to develop new modes of nonhierarchical organizations, and transparency and collaboration within women's studies.

The Feminist Press was one of the earliest allies that I found in my search, beginning collaborations that were intellectually stimulating and fascinating. They also forged many personal friendships which I shall value all my life. It was a joy to share responsibilities, resources, and ideas, learning from each other's particular concerns. They still remain living demonstrations of the growing base and solidarity of the international women's movement.

As I write this today, before me are reports of the Cairo Conference on Population and Development. They suggest that the North-South divide has resurfaced with a vengeance, aiding the forces of fundamentalism of many hues which stand opposed to the movement's goals. It is not only religious fundamentalisms which represent the inimical forces. Demographic fundamentalism, or the rise of the new scientific orthodoxy—which suppresses all voices of dissent within its own ranks, making, as the *Sunday Telegraph* reported, a scientist describe it as the new "population religion"—also threatens the future of the women's movement probably as much as the intolerance of critical interpretations of religious orthodoxy from a feminist or humanist perspective by individual authors.

Women's studies, feminist studies, women and development studies, have all in turn been called "the intellectual arms of the international women's movement." Many of us tried to use these "arms" to increase transparency and collaboration in our relationships and to increase our capacity to influence the world of international scholarship. When I hear the current buzzword of a "global civil society," my first reaction is to say that historically the internationalization of scholarship provided the first base for such a global civil society to emerge in the future.

But when I look at some of the current trends in the probing of cultural specificities, the growing jargonization and mystification, the essentialist view of culture, and a kind of territorialism and lack of transparency in the pursuit of such scholarship, I wonder how such feminist studies can continue to strengthen the women's movement at the global, national, or regional levels. I am not certain whether these are the genuine voices of feminism, or another brand of orthodoxy that can be easily manipulated by the powers that seek to divide all of us.

Does this all sound like a prophecy of doom? I like being called an "incorrigible optimist," and will stake my faith that feminism and the women's movement will survive these threats. To be forewarned is to be forearmed. The voices of democracy and cultural pluralism—not fossilized and frozen in a point of time—enriching each other through sharing and joining in the search for common human values will ultimately triumph. Our generation may not be here to see that day. But leadership will emerge from below, from the young, and the still invisible but now articulate majority. They will learn from our mistakes as well as our victories.

VINA MAZUMDAR, a political scientist and historian, is director emerita of the Center for Women's Development Studies in New Delhi, India. She contributed an afterword to *Seeds: Supporting Women's Work in the Third World* **(The Feminist Press, 1989).**

Celebrating Bold Innocents —Someone Forgot to Tell Us We Couldn't

Nellie Y. McKay

NINETEEN NINETY-FOUR AND 1995 ARE, FOR ME, TWO YEARS IN WHICH I CELEBRATE A NUMBER OF TWENTY-FIFTH ANNIVERSARIES, ALL OF THEM WONDERFUL. IN 1969 I WENT TO GRADUATE SCHOOL; IN 1970 THE FEMINIST PRESS WAS ESTABLISHED; AND IN 1969-1970 THE AFRO-AMERICAN STUDIES DEPARTMENT AT THE UNIVERSITY OF WISCONSIN-MADISON, A HOME WITHIN MY HOME, CAME INTO BEING. THE DECISION TO GO TO GRADUATE SCHOOL WAS MORE MOMENTOUS THAN I KNEW THEN, FOR IT HAS GIVEN ME A LIFE THAT, AT THAT TIME, I COULD NOT HAVE IMAGINED IN MY WILDEST DREAMS. BUT THEN I DID NOT KNOW THERE WAS A FEMINIST PRESS, AND WOULD NOT BECOME CONSCIOUSLY AWARE OF IT FOR SEVERAL YEARS. MEN OVERSHADOWED MY EARLY YEARS IN GRADUATE SCHOOL: OLD AND NOT-SO-OLD WHITE MEN, SELF-APPOINTED SOLE GUARDIANS OF ALL KNOWLEDGE, AND YOUNGER MEN WHO ASPIRED TO THEIR "THRONES"; WOMAN WAS INDEED CREATED FROM ADAM'S RIB; AND "FEMINIST" WAS AN ALMOST UNKNOWN WORD TO ME SINCE I DON'T RECALL IT FROM PRE-GRADUATE SCHOOL CONVERSATIONS WITH MY FRIENDS. HOW DIFFERENT MY WORLD IS TODAY! SINCE 1969, I'VE LEARNED THAT IN MY AUDACITY (A WORD I COULD NOT HAVE CONCEIVED FOR ME IN 1969 EITHER) TO BE IN THAT PLACE AT THAT TIME MADE ME SOMETHING I DID NOT KNOW I WAS: A FEMINIST, A BLACK FEMINIST. THEN TOO, TODAY THE FEMINIST PRESS IS A BELOVED INSTITUTION IN MY LIFE, TO VALUE, TO RESPECT, AND TO CELEBRATE: ONE WITH AN ANNIVERSARY I TOO CLAIM IN 1995. ONE FOR OUR SIDE.

In the late 1960s my social references were the Black Revolution, the Civil Rights movement, Martin Luther King Jr., black college students in rebellion in white colleges and universities in the north, on television, police dogs attacking unarmed southern blacks who dared to claim humanity, street demonstrations against racism and segregation, and a decade of blood that took the lives of the nation's brightest and best, whites and blacks alike. Certainly not the white feminist movement.

Putting aside an early ambition to be the first black woman Shakespearean to join the CUNY faculty, I went to graduate school to read American literature, the great American writers, the Hawthornes and the Melvilles, to learn what made America tick. As far as I knew, there were no great writers who were black men, and certainly no black women who wrote anything worth reading. I could not have dreamed how differently I would see the world and me in it in a short five years: How Barbara Christian, and Paule Marshall, and Toni Morrison, and Andrea Benton Rushing, and Alice Walker, and Mary Helen Washington, and a host of other women, black and white, writers and critics, women I know as friends and colleagues, and some I've never met, how our meetings, face-to-face and/or on the printed page, changed my life.

In 1978 I came to Madison to teach and learn to be a scholar, not of Shakespeare (whose work I still adore), or of Melville, or that great wordsmith William Faulkner, but of black American writers and particularly black American women writers. And in another once-unimaginable happening, I made Madison my home. This year, the Afro-American studies department here, the center of my home, celebrates the third of the twenty-fifth anniversaries in my life in 1994 and 1995. Old-timers tell stories of the department's rocky start; immodestly, I say, "I've helped to make it great." For the opportunity to have known and worked with others who also make it great, to the students who have come across my path (some of the best of whom, as difficult as this is for me to believe, aspire to *my* throne), and to an institution that supported me to help me find my own way in the lofty but thorny profession that I claim, I owe profound gratitude and revel in this twenty-fifth year anniversary as well. My world has indeed changed, and so have I.

In the early 1980s I left Madison for a year to complete the book that brought me tenure. Just before my departure, two male colleagues, one white, the other black, in a joking conversation in which I was not a participant but which they staged for my benefit, expressed relief because my leaving meant they could "go back to business as usual." They, of course, enjoyed my programmed retort. I thought: "Educating men is hard work." Shortly following my return, I was in a hallway conversation with a group of four or five male colleagues when they decided it was time to go to the Terrace (an outdoor extension of the Student Union on Lake Mendota) "to have a beer." A few minutes into their arrangement-making for this late afternoon's social time, I realized that no one had included me. In a voice that intimated black women's well-known "hands on hips" posture, I told them exactly what I thought of them. The rowdy outburst of spontaneous male laughter did not disguise (even to me) their discomfiture. The youngest of the group took instant flight, deserting his companions and calling loudly as he hurried down the hall: "See, I told you so, now you guys are in trouble again." They had been "back to business as usual."

"Educating" the men who came of age in a world where women were believed created from Adam's rib, in departments (as almost all academic departments are) still overshadowed by male presence, continues to be hard work at times, but much less so than it used to be. Now there are men who call themselves feminists, and others who behave as though they should. Even the worst of the "real" men have learned some new sensitivities. "Who could have imagined," Barbara Smith asked me a few years ago, "that courses on black women writers would ever enroll hundreds of students?" We could not. It is not male "business as usual" in either the English or the Afro-American studies departments where I work, nor is it for most of the men I interact with here and elsewhere. My world has changed, and although still full of shortcomings, many changes are for the good.

I remain aghast at how innocent I was in 1969, awed that even in that innocence I made the choices that I did. The Feminist Press and an indomitable Florence Howe together, a feminist success of grand proportions, came to be as a very bold adventure of innocent idealists at the same time that one (unknowingly) bold black woman, first on the family tree to enter the world of graduate school, walked across the threshold of an Ivy League university and toward an unimaginable future; and a group of young black and white students and untenured assistant professors, almost as innocent, were bold enough to move a mostly unmovable giant to make Afro-American studies a reality in Madison. We were all bold innocents who not only survived but triumphed, and in that triumph helped to forever change the face of American education.

Now less than a decade and a half beyond my first unpleasant encounters with some of my male colleagues, it is not "business as usual" in the places where we entered; fewer "guys" get into some of the kinds of trouble they once did. I claim my anniversaries all, take pride in celebrations of hard battles won, and raise a toast: One for all Bold Innocents, someone forgot to tell us we couldn't!

NELLIE Y. McKAY is professor of American and Afro-American studies and chair of the Afro-American studies department at the University of Wisconsin-Madison. She wrote afterwords to *The Changelings* by Jo Sinclair (The Feminist Press, 1985) and *Daddy Was a Number Runner* by Louise Meriwether (The Feminist Press, 1986).

Photo by Jeff Miller.

The Changing Face of Feminism

Toni McNaron

Twenty-five years ago, feminists were most often a collection of white, middle-class, heterosexual women and some closet lesbians working on issues of redress. Now the face of feminism has been altered permanently. Women of color, lesbians of all sorts, working-class, disabled, and older women are speaking our stories and making our theories. The basic question is no longer "Where were the women?" but "What kinds of resistance to racist and classist heterosexism have always been practiced by women within their various 'tribes' or communities?" Recent work on the role of the physical or sexual has enlivened feminist debate considerably. In fact, debate has become the hallmark of much of our current scholarly and pedagogical work. While this is a sign of internal strength, these debates can become dangerous weapons in the hands of enemies of women in the religious right and the capitalist mainstream, all of whom prefer their women only in the kitchen or bedroom.

Perhaps the single most challenging issue before feminists of any description is the frightening rise in acts of violence against women, be they rape and battery of wives and daughters or death threats against public lesbians. I see feminism's extending its theory and practice into virtually every corner of human existence in the coming decades, requiring of leaders as well as of intimates that they recognize women's autonomy and that they assent to words written almost two hundred years ago by Charlotte Brontë: "[Women] need exercise for their faculties, and a field for their efforts"; as well as those penned more recently by Toni Morrison: "Had she paints, or clay, or knew the discipline of the dance, or strings; had she anything to engage her tremendous curiosity and her gift for metaphor, she might have exchanged the restlessness and preoccupation with whim for an activity that provided her with all she yearned for. And like any artist with no art form, she became dangerous."

TONI McNARON teaches women's studies and English at the University of Minnesota-Minneapolis. She is author of *I Dwell in Possibility: A Memoir* (The Feminist Press, 1992).

Who Could Remain Untouched?

Ritu Menon

Little did I think in 1970 when we published Kate Millet's *Sexual Politics* at Doubleday (where I began my involvement with publishing) that a concern with women would fill my working and personal life as it has today. I can remember the excitement of reading Millet and knowing, almost intuitively, that this was going to trigger something irreversible, something momentus in the way that male-female relationships are understood. But me? Well, I'd never thought that I, personally, had been discriminated against as a woman, so unconscious was my internalization of social norms, so apparently smooth my passage from girlhood to womanhood. I had done what I wanted, gone where I chose, been "independent." Then why did what Millett was saying ring so true?

When I returned to India, my grandmother, "illiterate" and married at age twelve, said only one thing to me: "Don't ever give up working—keep your own destiny in the fist of your hand. You're fortunate to be educated. Look at me." I remembered my mother, highly educated for her time, wanting to work but actively discouraged by family and friends. My aunts, intelligent, talented, but subtly denied. Not unhappy, mind you, just unfulfilled. These were patriarchal attitudes, I began to realize.

I plunged into work. In mainstream publishing, the clear majority of books were by men, the publishing priorities were set by them, the marketplace controlled by them, the rules made by them. Women were accommodated—when the men decided. But things were changing. The seventies and eighties saw the burgeon-ing of the local and international women's movements, women's studies, the force of feminism. Who could remain untouched by them?

In 1984 we set up Kali for Women, Urvashi Butalia and I, and since then the vision has been an ever-widening one, rippling out to far horizons, focusing on what's close to home. And always learning, exploring, questioning, trying to understand, knowing that what we're doing, what we're publishing, is not just another job, but a project. A project for social change.

A vision, at once, old and new.

RITU MENON is copublisher of the Indian publishing house Kali for Women. She is an editor of *Truth Tales: Contemporary Stories by Women Writers of India* (The Feminist Press, 1990) and *Slate of Life: More Contemporary Stories by Women Writers of India* (The Feminist Press, 1994), both originally published by Kali for Women.

The Utterance

Robin Morgan

We have worked for a quarter century to name our pain and rage aloud—and now it is spoken. It should come as no surprise that what is at last heard will be at first disbelieved. But this time, no one can undo the utterance.

Because some of us have dared learn to read and write.

We have worked for a quarter of a century to articulate our vision for a transformed world. It should come as no surprise that our longing for sanity will be called madness, our pragmatism termed idealistic. But this time, no one can erase the vision.

They will try to deny it, denounce it, defuse it, rename it. They will label it "post-feminism," or the Gaia principle, or the Aquarian Age. They can call it anything they wish, but they can never again ignore it.

It is a woman in Oklahoma and in Florida, in Burma and in South Africa, in Montreal and Rio, naming herself. It is the female majority of the human species, moving to protect sentient life on this planet. It is the surfacing of the depths onto the shore, of the private into the public, of the hidden and despised into the light. It is the energy of action. It is the earth erupting. It is the people speaking.

It is us.

ROBIN MORGAN, activist and former editor in chief of *Ms.*, is a prize-winning writer and poet who has published fourteen books, including *Sisterhood is Powerful*, *Sisterhood is Global*, and *The Mer-Child: A Legend for Children and Other Adults* (The Feminist Press, 1991).

Photo by Sally Tagg.

Not a Cautionary Tale

Charlotte Nekola

TWENTY YEARS LATER, NOT BEING MAYA DEREN WAS SOMETHING I HAD TO ADMIT. IT CAME AS A SHOCK, AS DID SEEING MAYA DEREN'S HALLUCINATORY AVANT-GARDE FILM FROM THE 1940s, *MESHES OF THE AFTERNOON.*

The first time I saw Maya Deren's film, I was nineteen, attending a college film course. In the dark auditorium, I was working on an idea of the world as a historical mindscape, full of protest, the intricacies of psychoanalysis, the mocking questions of surrealism—the kind of world that my former "good" girl life in the suburbs was designed to studiously avoid. I had been expected to skim lightly over life, not to speak of anything like guilt or lust, despair or dreams. Now I was watching fourteen minutes of the most perfect black and white footage, a disturbing collage that raised many hard questions, and made by a woman.

Meshes of the Afternoon presents a short drama of mysterious images: woman, knife, sea, stairs, man, double of the same woman, a table, a mirror, a nun with the face of a mirror. A mean-sounding hum and occasional hollow drum music accompanies what we see. The woman dies, or kills herself, or is drowned, or dreams—it's hard to tell.

The film goes for only fourteen minutes, but because the images are suspended over such mystery, it seems more like four hours. Even more arresting than the nagging points of the story line are the questions raised by the mood—menace, fracture. Fractured gestures toward connection between the woman, the man, the nun, or the mirror only tear them apart. And, Maya Deren both directed and starred in her film—I had never heard of a woman like that, especially one who pushed dark thoughts out to the open edge of sunlight. Instantly, she became my bad girl heroine.

As a plus, in the movie, she wore the most perfectly fitting gabardine pants, trouser-like but ballooning, an improved version of what I thought adventurous women who riveted planes together on the homefront during World War II looked like. Exactly the kind of pants my girlfriends and I would have if we had our own film studio, or gas station, or airplane hangar.

Further, when I looked into her biography, it seemed she had pushed her own life to the edge as well as her work. In 1946, she went to Haiti to make a film on voodoo. She became so immersed in the study of voodoo that she found herself writing the first definitive study on it, a hefty tome called *Divine Horsemen*, still regarded as a landmark work.

Her chapter titles are as provocative as her film—"The White Darkness" or "The Cosmic Mirror and the Corpse on the Cross Road." Her book tells about her participation in voodoo rituals, when she lost her own subjectivity to the rites, when one leg suddenly rooted to the ground and the rest of her nearly fell away. Meanwhile, she piled up case after case of footage on voodoo rituals but could not bring herself to edit any of them. Then, suddenly, she died of a cerebral hemorrhage at age fifty-two.

Once I thought an excess of cerebration had literally killed her. She had allowed herself to think too much, about what we cannot know or say, about voodoo, I told myself. Now I can't believe this thought registered with me, almost as if I were saying that she got what she asked for. I see that I used to believe that thought could not be owned by a woman—despite her brilliant film, her erudition, or her perfect trousers—without a severe penalty.

Maya Deren's name, over the next twenty years, became a password, spoken between myself and woman friends reverentially, a little knowingly. We never talked about why. I took it that she occupied the same place in our collective consciousness, the woman who wasn't afraid of standing at the edge, who had probably even gone over. She did not have children. She was an absolute standard for "doing your work," which was a phrase we used to describe working your art, or writing, on top of the day job you might have, and the children that might be circling your feet. Maya Deren was a possibility, a line somewhere up on the horizon that we might approach.

The menacing music of her film hummed through our lives, up the stairwells of houses and universities, behind the sandwiches we wrapped for children. I had gathered children, students, houses, roads, and trees around me, not an extended overseas stay studying voodoo and a sudden death. Sometimes I would fight with my idea of Maya Deren, trying to justify my choices.

Only recently did it occur to me that I had read her film and life as a terrible parable, of how a woman might die from thinking, and that I had used this parable to limit my own scope. I had turned her visionary film and remarkable life into a cautionary tale, through a kind of self-censorship.

Months later I found out that many other women had adopted the Maya Deren password as well—a collective in California devotes itself to compiling a four-volume study of her life and work. They are up to Volume Two. And I am approaching my own Volume Two, in which I admit that I did not become Maya Deren, but there is no reason to try to drive her from my life. It is possible to move toward her line on the horizon, maybe not without penalty, but to move anyway. Twenty-five years later, it is now time to celebrate her work and life, and ours as well, without censoring the territory of brain, history, psyche, children, sex, or world that a woman may need to transverse.

CHARLOTTE NEKOLA, assistant professor of English at William Patterson College, coedited with Paula Rabinowitz *Writing Red: An Anthology of American Women Writers, 1930-1940* (The Feminist Press, 1987) and is author of *Dream House: A Memoir*.

Photo by Stephen Barker.

Focus on the Concepts

Mary Ann B. Oakley

FEMINISM TWENTY-FIVE YEARS LATER? A QUARTER OF A CENTURY AGO WE FEMINISTS WERE MUCH YOUNGER, MORE OPTIMISTIC, READY TO GRAB THE WORLD AND MOVE IT FORWARD. WE HAD SEEN THE LIGHT AND WE SET OUT TO CONVERT EVERYONE ELSE. IT IS INTERESTING THAT, AS WE HAVE GROWN OLDER AND OUR GOALS OF MAXIMIZING THE POTENTIAL OF EVERY WOMAN AND CREATING WIDER OPPORTUNITIES AND CHOICES ARE NOW SHARED BY SO MANY, "FEMINISM" HAS BECOME ALMOST A DIRTY WORD IN THIS DAY OF THE RADICAL RIGHT. PERHAPS WE NEED TO PUT ASIDE LABELS AND FOCUS THE CONCEPTS WHICH BIND WOMEN OF DIVERSE BACKGROUNDS AND INTERESTS TOGETHER. CERTAINLY WE NEED TO CONTINUE TO TEACH OUR CHILDREN, OF BOTH GENDERS, THAT THEY CAN GO AS FAR AS THEIR ABILITIES WILL ALLOW IF THEY USE THOSE ABILITIES WELL AND BELIEVE IN THEMSELVES.

MARY ANN B. OAKLEY is an employment discrimination and civil rights lawyer in Atlanta. She is author of *Elizabeth Cady Stanton* (The Feminist Press, 1972).

Excerpt from "Dream-Vision"*

Tillie Olsen

I HAD SEEN MY MOTHER BUT THREE TIMES IN MY ADULT LIFE, SEPARATED AS WE WERE BY THE CONTINENT BETWEEN, BY LACK OF MEANS, BY JOBS I HAD TO KEEP AND BY THE NEEDS OF MY FOUR CHILDREN. SHE COULD SCARCELY WRITE ENGLISH— HER ONLY EDUCATION IN THIS COUNTRY A FEW MONTHS OF NIGHT SCHOOL. WHEN AT LAST I FLEW TO HER, IT WAS IN THE LAST DAYS SHE HAD LANGUAGE AT ALL. TOO LATE TO TALK WITH HER OF WHAT WAS IN OUR HEARTS; OR OF HARMS AND CRUCIFYING AND STRENGTHS AS SHE HAD KNOWN AND EXPERIENCED THEM; OR OF WHYS AND KNOWLEDGE, OF WISDOM. SHE DIED A FEW WEEKS LATER.

She, who had no worldly goods to leave, yet left to me an inexhaustible legacy. Inherent in it, this heritage of summoning resources to make—out of song, food, warmth, expressions of human love—courage, hope, resistance, belief; this vision of universality, before the lessenings, harms, divisions of the world are visited upon it.

She sheltered and carried that belief, that wisdom—as she sheltered and carried us, and others—throughout a lifetime lived in a world whose season was, as it still is, a time of winter.

"Dream-Vision" originally appeared in Mother to Daughter, Daughter to Mother: A Feminist Press Daybook and Reader *(The Feminist Press, 1984).*

TILLIE OLSEN is the award-winning author of the story collection *Tell Me a Riddle*, the novel *Yonnonido*, and the volume *Silences*. She edited and contributed a biographical interpretation to *Life in the Iron Mills* by Rebecca Harding Davis (The Feminist Press, 1972) and compiled *Mother to Daughter, Daughter to Mother: A Feminist Press Daybook and Reader* (The Feminist Press, 1984).

Photo by Miriam Berkley.

Always Remember

Gloria F. Orenstein

GLORIA F. ORENSTEIN is professor of comparative literature in the Program for the Study of Women and Men in Society at the University of California, Los Angeles. She is completing a memoir for The Feminist Press to be published in 1996.

Photo by Irene Fertik.

As WE MOVE INTO THE TWENTY-FIRST CENTURY (THE THIRD MILLENIUM OF THE COMMON ERA), AND AS I REFLECT UPON THE REVOLUTIONARY WAY IN WHICH ALL KNOWLEDGE OF THE "*HISTORY OF MAN*KIND" HAS BEEN OVERTHROWN BY CONTEMPORARY FEMINIST SCHOLARSHIP (THAT HAS ONLY BEEN SYSTEMATICALLY DEVELOPED OVER THE PAST TWO DECADES), I AM MOVED TO SAY THIS TO THE YOUNG WOMEN OF THE FUTURE: ALWAYS REMEMBER—ALL THE DATA ISN'T IN YET! THEY HAVE EXCAVATED ONLY ONE THIRTY-SECOND OF CATAL HUYUK, THE NEOLITHIC GODDESS CENTER OF ANATOLIA, TURKEY!

For me, the most dramatic re-visioning of women's history came about via the archaelogical revelations made by Marija Gimbutas in her monumental scholarly works on the pre-patriarchal Goddess civilization of "Old Europe" and by the daring historical and theological re-visioning by Merlin Stone in *When God Was a Woman*.

To understand that for millenia humans lived in gender-egalitarian cultures that had no weapons, and that they revered nature and communed with The Great Creator of All Life in the sacred image of a female is to be given the gift of Hope. This empowering knowledge that came to me via women's studies bestowed upon all women, not only the gift of hope for survival, but also for the reflowering of a possible ecofeminist culture on planet Earth for now and in the future.

We must always remember to document the multiple achievements and creations of our foremothers around the world, and we must never forget that the Earth is our first Mother without whose fruits of abundance we would perish. We must continually acknowledge and give thanks for Her all-nurturing Cornucopia.

It is also vitally important to the future of feminism to learn to think through all our decisions to seven generations into the future (as the indigenous peoples of the world have taught us) as well as to remember our ancestors for at least seven generations into the past.

In this way we can ensure the connection of our roots to our new flowering, and we can provide for the sturdy "gyn/ecological" constitution of our new "feminist matristic"* Tree of Life.

"Feminist matristic" is a concept that I coined in The Reflowering of the Goddess *to link our contemporary feminist consciousness to our roots in ancient matristic (goddess-centered) cultures.*

From Invisibility to Hyper-Visibility

Nell Irvin Painter

TWENTY-FIVE YEARS AGO! MY STUDENTS WEREN'T BORN, MY COLLEAGUES WERE TOTS! COME TO THINK OF IT, I WAS PRETTY YOUNG, TOO, IN THE MIDDLE OF AN ON-AGAIN, OFF-AGAIN GRADUATE CAREER IN AFRICA, CALIFORNIA, ENGLAND, AND MASSACHUSETTS. I HAD ONLY JUST EMBARKED ON THE LAST LAP OF MY JOURNEY IN GRADUATE SCHOOL, IN CAMBRIDGE.

In the fall of 1969 I was isolated in seminars in the Harvard history department, where I carried the burden of all people of color (even Turks!) in every meeting. I was surrounded by preening white men who assumed that the sun rose only for them. This was still the 1960s, remember, before the recession of the mid-1970s that blighted so many of their chances. They knew that upon graduation they'd take their anointed places at the head of the historical profession.

Moi? I was something else. First of all, as I discovered in Cambridge, I was a westerner—from Oakland, California. This counted against me mostly among the other African-American students, who coolly but pointedly ranked each other's Vineyard points and eastern network placement. (White people, male and female, for the most part, didn't get past race.) But I had experiences in interesting places and could speak foreign languages better than most. This located me not above, but off to the side in the history department and the Harvard community. In those days, white women were not sisters. They didn't become sisters until they stopped ignoring me and other black women and our work—long about the mid-1980s.

But rather than talk about isolation from white women, let me point out some notable exceptions: The Feminist Press was always open to women of color, and that mission has been wonderfully permanent. And once the Berkshire Women's History Conference reinvented itself, those in charge groped toward diversity. I was on the program committee for the 1976 Big Berks meeting, and though I felt like a freak, I was there. Gerda Lerner took an early interest in my work and my career, and my feminist colleagues at the University of Pennsylvania, where I had my first job in the 1970s, tried awkwardly to extend a hand. That hand wasn't much of a help to me at the time. In hindsight I see that those women did make an effort in an otherwise hostile environment.

For many years I worked in what felt like invisibility. I wrote and wrote, yet colleagues didn't use or cite my work. Then all of a sudden I became hyper-visible and my name appeared in everyone's papers. Partly it's my being at Princeton, where the spotlight shines more brightly than at a state institution in the south. But also it's my writing on a black woman (Sojourner Truth) that seems to make people feel better. There still exists a gut-level conviction that scholars need to write out of their bodies, and that my writing about all Americans, as in *Standing at Armageddon*, somehow wasn't as authentic, as valued, as my writing about Sojourner Truth.

After Sojourner Truth, I will again be writing about the tangled interrelationship of whites and blacks in American culture: I don't see that segregating one's history follows logically from many Americans' former conviction that the color line was a right and natural thing. Years from now we'll see how well my readers are able to focus on that new project. Let's see how much has changed in the gendering and racializing of scholarship since 1969, 1979, and 1989, when the scholar is, as we say, differently situated.

NELL IRVIN PAINTER, Edwards Professor of American History at Princeton University, is author of the forthcoming *Sojourner Truth: A Life, a Symbol*. She wrote the introduction to Jacqueline Bernard's *Journey Toward Freedom* (The Feminist Press, 1990).

Conversations*

Grace Paley

MY HUSBAND'S MOTHER LIVED IN FLORIDA ON THE SANDY SHORE OF A SMALL LAKE IN THE MIDDLE OF AN ORANGE GROVE THAT LOOKED SOMETHING LIKE A CHILD'S PAINTING, BASED IN THE COLOR OF SAND WITH AN OCCASIONAL SPEAR OF GREEN GREEN GRASS BENDING THIS WAY AND THAT. SHE WAS DYING AND WANTED TO ASK A COUPLE OF QUESTIONS ABOUT LIFE. WE COULD SPEAK TO HER ONLY AT LUNCH—BRIEFLY—AND LATER AT SUPPER. SHE DIDN'T EAT MUCH BUT IT WAS THE HOUR OF HER LITTLE STRENGTH AND SHE OFFERED IT TO US.

One evening at supper she asked me about Women's Lib. She and her best friend (also very sick) had been talking about it. She said she thought I might know something about it. What was it like? Did it mean there would be women lawyers?

Yes.

Would they work for women?

Oh surely, I said.

Would women get paid the same? Was that the idea?

One of them, I answered. Equal pay at least.

Would women be free of men bossing them around?

Hopefully, I said. Though it might take the longest amount of time since it would involve lots of changes in men.

Oh they won't like that a bit, she said. Would people love their daughters then as much as their sons?

Maybe more, I said.

Not fair again, she said slyly.

But that wasn't all, I said. Most of the Womens Libbers I knew really didn't want to have a piece of the men's pie. They thought that pie was kind of poisonous, toxic, reallyfull of weapons, poison gasses, all kinds of mean junk we didn't even want a slice of.

She was tired. That's a lot she said. Then she went upstairs to sleep.

In the morning she surprised us. She came down for breakfast. I couldn't sleep she said. I was up all night thinking of what you said. You know she said, there isn't a thing I've done in my life that I haven't done for some man. Dress up or go out or take a job or quit it or go home or leave. Or even be quiet or say something nice, things like that. You know I was up all night thinking about you and especially those young women. I couldn't stop thinking about what wonderful lives they're going to have.

This story first appeared in Long Walks and Intimate Talks *(The Feminist Press, 1991).*

GRACE PALEY is a prizewinning author whose most recent book, *The Collected Stories*, was nominated for the National Book Award. Her other books include *The Collected Poems* and *Long Walks and Intimate Talks*, a collaborative work with Vera B. Williams of stories, poems, and paintings (The Feminist Press, 1991).

Equality across Boundaries

Hanna Papanek

IN MY VISION OF FEMINISM AROUND THE WORLD IN THE NEXT TWENTY-FIVE YEARS, I LOOK AHEAD WITH THE CONVICTION THAT WE MUST NOT FORGET THE PAST IN OUR EFFORTS TO MOVE FORWARD, AND WE MUST REMEMBER WHAT BRINGS US TOGETHER AS MUCH AS WHAT MAKES US DIFFERENT. AS I NOW THINK BACK TO MY OWN PAST OF MANY IMPOSED AND CHOSEN EXILES, I TRY TO EXAMINE WHAT I HAVE LEARNED IN EACH OF THESE EXILES AND WHAT THE SUM TOTAL NOW MEANS TO ME.

Feminism came very naturally in a life begun among many caring women and a few loving men, where my family's democratic socialist ideology not only shaped how we lived with each other but also gave us a solid grounding for dealing with the exigencies of life in many exiles, sometimes in great poverty. Later I sometimes chose temporary exile in another culture as part of my work and my life, so I could learn about similarities and differences, repeating and revalidating aspects of my past.

As a feminist intellectual who has experienced exile, I have also learned that intellectuals in exile have special responsibilities, regardless of the specific causes of their exile. They—we—must strive, by an act of will and choice, to become part of the world's conscience. As persons who have absorbed more than one social structure, we can struggle to develop a different perspective embodying elements of these different cultures that is nevertheless unique and personal.

This is also why my life as an exile has made me impatient with the barriers imposed by political forces, language, politics, racial and cultural differences. I seek a mutually respectful equality across these boundaries, an understanding among individuals that does not overlook the differences among our groups but also does not glorify them so much that they become barriers. For those of us who are feminist scholars who sometimes work with colleagues in other societies, this vision of our role as unarguable equals is a crucial precondition of our work. Our work together reaffirms the possibility of boundary crossing by all those who choose it.

In the international women's movement, the goals of many individuals and groups come into contact and sometimes into conflict. I am convinced that this conflict is best resolved not by raising even higher the barriers encoded in differences of class, culture, race, and language but by finding boundary-crossing paths that respect identities on all sides. I cannot believe that identities are best achieved by the exclusion of alternatives. Even

if a turning inward is occasionally necessary for a person or a group, it needs to alternate with an outward look, a crossing of borders done willingly and without compulsion. In my vision of a future feminism, this balance will have been achieved.

HANNA PAPANEK was a 1993-1994 Bunting Institute Fellow and Visiting Scholar at the Center for European Studies at Harvard University. She is codirector with Vina Mazumdar of research on Women's Work and Family Strategies in South and Southeast Asia and she wrote the afterword to *Sultana's Dream* by Rokeya Sakhawat Hossain (The Feminist Press, 1988).

Photo by Martha Stewart.

Gains and Losses

Amanda Powell

"THE FEMINISM OF THE FUTURE?"—I WRITE THIS *TIRED*, HERE IN OREGON, FACING YET ANOTHER ATTEMPT BY THE SO-CALLED CHRISTIAN RIGHT TO POLICE, STIFLE, AND CRIMINALIZE SEXUALITY—HOMOSEXUALITY FIRST, AND THEN, WHO KNOWS? THESE ASSAULTS HIT AT MY CREATIVE, SCHOLARLY, AND PROFESSIONAL AS WELL AS PERSONAL LIFE.

I hope the feminism of the future will be historically aware of our past, able to claim a more diverse and complex history of women's accomplishments and struggles. Literary and historical work on the pre-nineteenth-century past of Europe and the Americas usefully undoes any simple notion of "progress" in women's history. Time and again there have been some gains, and there have been some losses.

Sex itself has not always everywhere been the phobic site that it is in this Anglo-puritan culture. In much twentieth-century feminist thinking and activism, a sense of "history" has extended only as far back as the nineteenth, at most late eighteenth century. There has been a hegemony of post-enlightenment outlook, heavily puritan and Victorian. This still (even after the "sex wars" of the 1980s) contributes to a feminist squeamishness about sex and sexualities which complicates some of our most important confrontations: about population and reproduction, about sexual orientation, and about sexual harassment issues. Let's reclaim a womanly power that is more queer and proud of it!

At the same time, let's reclaim spirituality, in its formal as well as alternative manifestations. As we do so, we need to consider the ways that women have always been involved in its institutional forms—churches, synagogues, mosques, et cetera. Many women today are to be found involved in mainstream as well as less numerous faith traditions. To ignore their contributions, concerns, and experiences deeply undermines our movement. As we search the past for what we can use now, we will certainly need to identify what's not so useful: accepting, not condemning or pretending it hasn't happened. In exploring a women's history of all classes and races, let's take women where they are, not excluding politically incorrect or even downright embarrassing women. They may be exactly whom we need to hear from.

AMANDA POWELL is a poet and translator who teaches Spanish/Latin American language and literature at the University of Oregon. She is co-editor and cotranslator with Electa Arenal of *The Answer/La Respuesta* by Sor Juana Inés de la Cruz (The Feminist Press, 1994).

Photo by Annette Gurdjian.

Edna's Complaint and Mine

Paula Rabinowitz

I GAVE MY COPY OF *THE AWAKENING* THIS SUMMER TO A WOMAN FROM MONTREAL, A SCHOOLTEACHER BIKING FROM CANADA TO CONNECTICUT, WHOM I MET AT LAKE ST. CATHERINE IN VERMONT. THIS CHEAP AVON PAPERBACK EDITION THAT HAD SAT ON MY SHELF FOR ALMOST TWENTY-FIVE YEARS SEEMED PERFECT BEACH READING—A STORY OF ANOTHER WOMAN SUMMERING AT THE BEACH WITH HER TWO CHILDREN. BUDGET CUTS HAVE ELIMINATED LIFEGUARDS AT VERMONT STATE PARKS SO I HAVE USUALLY HAD TO WATCH MY SONS WITH HAWK EYES AS THEY EDGED EVER DEEPER INTO THE MILFOIL, ITS WEEDY TENTACLES THREATENING TO PULL THEM UNDER. BUT THIS YEAR MY CHILDREN BECAME SWIMMERS. WHEN I WASN'T SWIMMING OUT DEEP, I WOULD READ ABOUT A WOMAN WHO WAS. BESIDES, I HADN'T READ THIS CHERISHED FEMINIST CLASSIC, ONCE SO IMPORTANT TO ME, IN YEARS. I CARTED IT EVERY DAY ALONG WITH SHOVELS AND PAILS, GOGGLES AND PRETZELS, BUT I COULD BARELY GET THROUGH THE FIRST HALF. SO WHEN THIS AMAZON WITH A FRENCH ACCENT SAID SHE NEEDED SOMETHING TO READ, I PASSED IT ON.

I just couldn't stand Edna, her malaise beyond my sympathy. "What the hell is she complaining about?" I screamed at my friend when she arrived one steamy weekend with her two kids. Edna Pontellier had a husband who worked all week so she could pursue *l'affaire du coeur*, arriving each Friday evening, pockets loaded with bonbons for his children. Sure, she had the kids, but at least one, sometimes two, young black women tended their needs—fed, dressed, amused them so that Edna saw them only when it pleased her. Plus, a sexy young man flirted with her all summer while she lazed on an island in the Gulf—all meals included.

But wait, I'm forgetting her troubled soul-searching for something more than motherhood: An artistic spirit, she scans the horizon seeing fields of Kentucky bluegrass remembered from her childhood. Edna wavers between two visions of Creole womanhood—the indulgent mother and the ascetic artist—neither of which can fully accommodate her longings. She desires escape—and the sea ultimately provides it, not as a landscape but as a death scene.

Truthfully, I hated the bitch. And the corrosive atmosphere, the mystique of invisible suffering, suffusing the book. I couldn't finish her story, knowing her end and the book's left those two empty shells—her "antagonists"—orphaned for no good reason. Here I was sitting everyday at the beach with my two boys— no husband arriving like clockwork with brimming pockets; no one shopping, cooking, cleaning for me; no young man trailing me—yet I continue writing mired as I am in the chores of daily living. My story is replicated in one form or another by virtually every mother I know. Why did we think this self-indulgent woman oppressed? How come it has taken this feminist critic years to read the novel as a racist tract which conforms to every stereotype about whiteness and womanhood and work of postbellum America? Why has this book ever been read as a feminist classic? True, it poses an intriguing narrative problem, one which Virginia Woolf took up in *To the Lighthouse* and Tess Slesinger explored in *The Unpossessed*: how to be a woman, a mother, an artist. Like Chopin, these later authors could not envision a plot to chart this contradiction of fictions—its ability to imagine beyond limited stories, limited subjects.

Edna's malaise is acute, her complaints muted, precisely because she is so ignorant of the workings of her world. So full of insights, why can't she consider how her free time is purchased by others' labor? That artistic sensibility might thrive on physicality and the hard work of raising children not to mention earning a living? How her husband's commerce she finds so hideous actually propels her desires? Virtually none of this is speculated on in the novel—yet it rides along quietly in the back seat, like Edna's black servants, silently subsumed by the pressing demands of the main character. That is what so infuriated me this time around. Chopin hints at her awareness of the racism her novel promotes; in fact, her other works deal explicitly with the sexual, class, and race dynamics superintending southern life at the turn of the century. But it is veiled here, as if a declaration of feminist independence must give unwitting voice to whiteness and wealth. No wonder we are struggling to this day with that legacy of white women's complaints called feminism. Still, Edna's pain is palpable and Chopin sounded the silent cries middle-class women suppress; could she have found another way out than tragic or mythic merger with huge, dangerous, implacable nature?

Learning to swim is one of the landmark events of childhood. Each one—walking, talking, reading, biking, swimming, and (recently) driving—connected either to mobility or language, the ability to roam and return to tell about one's wonderings, one's wanderings. Edna learns to swim during her summer on Grand Isle, painting her visions of the newly-tamed sea. She might have held onto its contradictory invitation and listened more carefully to the Spanish girl tossing comments on the ferry, her servants' whispers, the bustle on the streets outside her enclosed house in the French Quarter, even her parrot's screeches, but she remains isolated. Her solitary gestures of freedom and defiance and desperation left two motherless children and many blank canvases.

Twenty-five years ago, we thought, "Oh yes, that's how it was then—and now." Today, when Thelma and Louise do little more than update Edna's fatal swim—this time by convertible and together without leaving small children behind—I think maybe we've learned something. Not enough, though. Imagine a story in which it is possible for women to be mothers and artists and take care of their business, leaning on the backs of others when they welcome us, sharing the beach and the streets and the stubby fingers sticky with melted chocolate.

PAULA RABINOWITZ is associate professor of English at the University of Minnesota-Minneapolis. She is coeditor with Charlotte Nekola of *Writing Red: An Anthology of American Women Writers, 1930-1940* (The Feminist Press, 1987).

Photo by Art Schwartz.

From the Scientific Front

Betty Rosoff and Ethel Tobach

At a meeting of the Association for Women in Science in 1975, Ethel Tobach and Betty Rosoff met again after thirty years and discussed some developments in the scientific community that were helping to perpetuate discrimination against women. First, it was being proposed that the genes on the X and Y chromosomes programmed men to be better fit for leadership roles in science and society. Second, there was an immediate and widespread acceptance of sociobiology, purporting to explain human behavior by the drive of the gene to pass itself on into the next generation. We decided that there was a need to develop valid scientific theory to fight these ideas. Thus, a group of people from various scientific disciplines, at all stages of scholarly training, and from nonacademic as well as academic work formed the Genes and Gender Collective. The Collective recognized that theory without practice would not be sufficient, and that it was necessary to have people of all ages, color, and gender contribute their knowledge and experience.

To do this we organized conferences, participated in scientific meetings, and published books in which we exposed the ways in which continuing attempts to misuse new knowledge about genetic processes were being made to continue the exploitation of women and people of color. During that time, the feminist movement became more aware of the concept of genetic determinism and engaged in theoretical and practical struggles through organizations and scholarship. At the same time, behavior geneticists, biologists, psychologists, and popular writers who espoused sociobiology were given credibility and prominence in the scientific community and society. These sociobiological scientists were and are being used by those who destroy the gains of feminists and people of color.

Genes and Gender has always integrated the struggles for racial, gender, and economic equity, and this approach is now part of feminist ideology and activity. Society's problems and crises, such as unemployment and global resource destruction, are accompanied by distortions and misapplications of science to justify exploitation, requiring feminists and all people of color to continually engage in the exposure of pseudoscience and its expression in policy.

Growth of feminist leadership in scientific organizations and on campuses along with the development of feminist theory promise to further the struggle for equality. The Genes and Gender Collective will continue to participate through the dissemination of scientific knowledge and research.

BETTY ROSOFF is an endocrinologist and professor emerita of biology at Stern College. ETHEL TOBACH is a comparative psychologist, curator emerita at the American Museum of Natural History, and adjunct professor of biology and psychology at the Graduate Center, CUNY. The Feminist Press has published Volumes VI and VII of the Genes and Gender series, *On Peace, War, and Gender* (1991) and *Challenging Racism and Sexism* (1994).

Disability Feminism

Marsha Saxton

THE ESSENCE OF FEMINISM IS EACH WOMAN REALIZING THAT SHE BELONGS IN THE CENTER OF THE COMMUNITY OF WOMEN AND IN THE CENTER OF THE COMMUNITY OF THE WORLD, LEARNING THAT HER INDIVIDUAL LIFE AND UNIQUE PERSPECTIVES ARE AN IMPORTANT CONTRIBUTION TO THE WHOLE. EACH WOMAN'S EXPERIENCES HELP GIVE ALL OF US A CLEARER AND MORE DETAILED PICTURE OF THE POWER AND PRIDE WE CAN TAKE IN BEING FEMALE.

We must be inclusive, open, and welcoming. We cannot judge any woman as having "arrived" at a particular level of awareness or power, which makes her a "feminist." This defeats the crucial notion that all women, wherever or however they live now, are the ones we most want to include and learn from.

Narrower definitions of feminism have tended to exclude women with disabilities. Some feminists imply that women with disabilities cannot be "real feminists" if we can't meet traditional feminist stereotypes, if we cannot be powerful, autonomous, highly intelligent, financially or physically independent. These notions hurt and limit all women, but especially have kept women with disabilities disconnected from the feminist community.

As women or girls with disabilities, we have particular insights and experiences we bring to the community, unique views of what it means to be female. This is the *disability feminism* we can offer to each other and to all females. As disabled women, we may need assistance in daily living activities, such as dressing, bathing, preparing and eating meals, communicating, moving, getting places. These experiences of "dependence," viewed through the veil of oppression, tend to portray the need for help as a burden to others. But we can also choose to regard this "dependence" as intimacy, as opportunities for close, wonderful collaboration with our family members or friends, or our paid attendants. We can begin to realize that the effort made to include us is as useful to our helpers as it is to us.

These are important lessons for nondisabled people who may live whole lives within the illusion that humans are separate, autonomous, isolated. Interdependence is essential and unavoidable for anyone who hopes to live a full life, not only because aging entails dependence on others, but because anyone who knows and cares for young children seeks to vali-date the needs of our young to feel unconditionally loved and accepted just as they are. Comfort with interdependence is fundamental for everyone who is human, and who, almost by definition, may need help at any time.

We must not confuse the value of helping disabled people with the traditional devaluing of women in the caregiver role. Women can indeed be overwhelmed and oppressed by the work of caring for loved ones who have disabilities. This is *not caused by the disabilities of those needing help*, but is the result of sexism and isolation inflicted on women caregivers. Any work, if sufficiently shared and validated, can become meaningful, important, and joyful.

Disability feminism regards our disabled young, infants, and girls with disabilities as precious and essential members of the community. These little ones are our community's future and deserve our attention and encouragement to regard themselves as deeply valued and magnificently female.

Women with disabilities may have experienced significant loss of body parts, or limitation in physical or mental function. A disabled woman's body may be unusual in appearance and judged as unattractive by cultural standards. Disabled women and girls may live in pain, may cost the community extra money, may die young. We know more than most other groups of women that "women can't do everything." Through the process of personal empowerment, we come to realize, and then to communicate to others, that our lives are worth the effort, that we are beautiful just as we are, that we are wonderfully female.

Oppression compels us to try to hide or deny some parts of ourselves: our different bodies, unusual minds, and unique ways of being. Reclaiming and with pride presenting all these parts of ourselves is a great gift to all women.

MARSHA SAXTON, founder of the Project on Women and Disability at the Massachussetts Office on Disability, is a consultant, trainer, and organizer in women's health and disability rights. She is a board member of the Boston Women's Health Book Collective and is coeditor with Florence Howe of *With Wings: An Anthology of Literature by and about Women with Disabilities* (The Feminist Press, 1987).

Photo by Flint Born.

The Kenning

Alix Kates Shulman

IN HER BOOK *HIPPARCHIA'S CHOICE*, THE FRENCH FEMINIST PHILOSOPHER MICHELLE LE DOUEFF DEVELOPS A USEFUL CONCEPT FOR ASSESSING THE RELATIONSHIP BETWEEN HOW FAR WE'VE COME AND HOW FAR WE'RE GOING. SHE WRITES:

Seventeenth-century English seafarers had a word to refer to the furthest visible point, corresponding to about twenty sea miles: the "kenning."…The kenning we need to give ourselves in politics is that of a generation: What should I be, do, demand, imagine today so that those who are now being born will from their earliest years discover an adult world in which some questions are being settled, so they can see different ones? If we could establish today that all authorities or decision-making bodies should be composed of equal numbers of men and women, sexism would very probably disappear from school textbooks. What a generation brought up in such a context could then think, what a truly mixed Parliament could concoct in the way of legislation are things that I cannot myself imagine because they go beyond my kenning.

The horizon is a moving orbit. Already, because of feminism, many women today face prospects (for work, education, family) far freer than those my generation was born to, though in other ways (disparities between rich and poor, violence, environmental dangers, for example) things seem worse than ever. Knowing that young feminists already see a somewhat different world than I see (as my most vivid memories fade to history for them), still, I celebrate the very plasticity, or *movement*, that makes this possible—especially since one fact seems to light up the entire past twenty-five years: *There are no ex-feminists.* Ex-communists, ex-Republicans, ex-Catholics, ex-Moonies, ex-hippies, ex-convicts, ex-lovers. But as far as I know, no ex-feminists. Evidently, once that feminist light goes on it gleams so fiercely you sometimes almost wish you could turn it off and take a nap. But hardly anyone does. However frustrating the inevitable twenty-mile limit of our kenning, it *moves*, taking into its sweep new realms of consciousness to map and mold. That so much remains to be done means tremendous opportunity: Just go out of your door in the morning and something crucial will present itself.

As Rabbi Tarfon said centuries ago, "You are not required to complete the task, but neither are you free to abandon it." Thus, feminism moves.

ALIX KATES SHULMAN is a writer whose books include *Memoirs of an Ex-Prom Queen* and a new memoir, *Drinking the Rain*. She will be writing a foreword for *The Little Locksmith* by Katharine Butler Hathaway, to be published by The Feminist Press in 1996.

Photo by Susan Wittenberg.

Confident

Dorothy Sterling

AS A PREMATURE FEMINIST WHO FIRST SPOKE FOR WOMEN'S RIGHTS IN ELEMENTARY SCHOOL IN THE 1920S WHEN THE BOYS WERE TAUGHT SCIENCE AND THE GIRLS SEWING, I CAN ONLY MARVEL AT THE ENORMOUS STRIDES THAT WOMEN HAVE MADE IN THE LAST TWENTY-FIVE YEARS. I WISH I COULD BE AROUND TO SEE WHAT THE NEXT TWENTY-FIVE WILL BRING, BUT I AM CONFIDENT THAT THE FUTURE—AND THE FUTURE OF THE FEMINIST PRESS—IS IN GOOD HANDS.

DOROTHY STERLING, a pioneer in African-American history and women's history, is the author of more than thirty books, including *Black Foremothers: Three Lives* (The Feminist Press, 1979; second edition 1988). She also contributed the introduction to *Turning the World Upside Down: The Anti-Slavery Convention of American Women Held in New York City, May 9-12, 1837* (The Feminist Press, 1987).

Questioning, Learning, Reading, Marching into the Year 2000

Amy Swerdlow

THE BIRTH OF THE FEMINIST PRESS TWENTY-FIVE YEARS AGO COINCIDED WITH MY OWN REBIRTH AS A FORTY-SIX-YEAR-OLD "YOUNG FEMINIST" DEEPLY ENGAGED IN RETHINKING MY POLITICS AND EVERYTHING ELSE. IN THOSE MAGICAL EARLY YEARS OF THE 1970S, WHEN THE WORLD SEEMED NEW AND MALLEABLE, FEMINIST PRESS BOOKS AND PAMPHLETS, WHICH WERE ALREADY CIRCULATING WIDELY IN THE FEMINIST COMMUNITY BEYOND ACADEME, INTRODUCED ME TO SOMETHING I HAD NEVER HEARD OF, BUT WAS WAITING FOR ALL MY LIFE. IT WAS THE ACADEMIC FIELD OF WOMEN'S STUDIES. IT DIDN'T TAKE ME LONG TO ENROLL IN A GRADUATE PROGRAM IN WOMEN'S HISTORY AFTER A HIATUS OF THIRTY YEARS DEVOTED TO MOTHERHOOD, A COMMUNITY ARTS CENTER, AND PEACE PROTEST.

Through the years of graduate school, The Press was a special source of inspiration and enlightenment. Florence Howe, always the scholar/activist/feminist entrepreneur, and later friend, knowing little of me save my work in the peace movement, invited me, *sans* credentials, to serve on the Reprints Advisory Board. The day-long meetings with the likes of Mary Jo Buhle, Elaine Hedges, Louis Kampf, Joan Kelly, and Catharine Stimpson filled me with awe, delight, and pride in my new calling. My work with The Press on the Women's Studies International project at the Women's Decade Conference in Copenhagen in 1980 and in Nairobi in 1985 were not only high points of my own political life, but the most significant points of reference for me, even now, in assessing feminist theory and practice.

Today in my emerita status, still striving to make a difference for women of my generation and for my daughters and granddaughters, the call of The Feminist Press to "Re-Vision Feminism Around the World" prompts me to move on with a "task to be done" I had already jotted down in my personal planner. However, my view of re-visioning feminism at this historic moment, as well as that of a number of other women's studies scholars of varied political, social, racial, ethnic, and religious backgrounds with whom I have been meeting in a Rutgers University Seminar on Global Women's Studies Curriculum Development, is more modest than that of The Press. Our aim is not so much to re-vision feminism around the world as to place U.S. feminism in a context of global interdependence. In so doing most of us will, of course, have to reconceptualize feminist theory and our own practice.

What we need in the immediate future is for The Feminist Press to provide us, as it has already begun to do, with the resources to perceive and comprehend better the lives and consciousness of women in other cultures, regions, and societies. We need to understand how women in other parts of the world see us both politically and culturally, how our actions and inactions affect them, and how the economic and cultural forces that control their lives also impact on ours.

This does not mean that we should, as one of the members of the Rutgers seminar put it recently, become intellectual tourists sinking in a sea of relativism, but rather we need to recognize our own location—socially, culturally, economically, and regionally, our own limitations of perception and agency, our responsibilities and possibilities for making meaningful connections with other women engaged in the global struggle for survival, for rights, and for joy. We should not be seeking a unified feminist theory at this historical moment, but rather for an understanding of where U.S. feminists situate ourselves in a complicated and racist global system. The Feminist Press is already taking a leading role in helping us to develop this global perspective that neither universalizes our own situation, nor is paralyzed by the multiplicity of differences and conflicts. Our task is not easy: Deepening our understanding of the lives and achievements and problems of all women, as well as defining our methods and goals are a first step. It's reassuring to know that our old friend and enabler, The Feminist Press, is already on the path, and that it will stay with us on our journey.

AMY SWERDLOW, professor emerita of history and director of the women's studies program at Sarah Lawrence College, is coauthor with Renate Bridenthal, Joan Kelly, and Phyllis Vine of *Families in Flux* (The Feminist Press, 1981; second edition, 1989).

Photo by Jan Hoffer.

Our Daughters Will Lead Us

Stephanie L. Twin

*O*UT OF THE BLEACHERS WAS DEDICATED TO MY DAUGHTER ALEXANDRA, WHO WAS ABOUT THREE WHEN THE BOOK APPEARED. HER SISTER DANIELLE WAS BORN SOON AFTER. TODAY, THESE GIRLS ARE BOTH YOUNG WOMEN AND I SEE IN THEM THE FUTURE OF FEMINISM.

The young women of their generation are self-directed; they have, or are searching for, goals reflecting their own true selves instead of men to create goals for them. How different from my mother's generation, when a woman's value was measured by her husband, or from my generation, which grew up expecting but not wanting to be traditional and then found ourselves pioneering a whole new way. Ask any young woman these days what she sees for her future and she'll tell you what profession she hopes to enter, what business she will open one day, or what creative art she wants to pursue. And of course, she'll add secondarily, she hopes to get married and have kids, or get married and not have kids, or just have kids, forget getting married, or just have a relationship, forget getting married or having kids. Any of these answers is quite remarkable, in light of women's history. I asked my daughter Danielle, now sixteen, how she would describe her generation. She wrote, "These girls know who they are, know what they want, and know how to get it without having to exploit themselves or their artistic expression." Well said.

So, when you ask, "Whither and how goest feminism, and who will lead us into its future?" the answer is, it is fine and strong and our daughters will lead us, for they have incorporated feminism into the fabric of their beings and their lives.

STEPHANIE L. TWIN is an independent consultant for not-for-profit and government organizations. She is author of *Out of the Bleachers: Writings on Women and Sport* (The Feminist Press, 1979).

Heaven Belongs to You*

Alice Walker

I WAS TALKING THIS AFTERNOON TO MY FRIEND, THE DIRECTOR OF *WARRIOR MARKS*, PRATIBHA PARMAR, WHO LIVES IN LONDON. SHE TOLD ME THAT THE WIFE OF OUR DRIVER, WHILE WE WERE FILMING IN AFRICA, WAS RECENTLY IN BRITAIN. AND THAT SHE WAS DISTRAUGHT BECAUSE HER HUSBAND, WHOM WE HAD ALL LIKED SO MUCH, AND WHO WAS VERY AWARE OF THE DANGERS AND PAIN INVOLVED IN FEMALE GENITAL MUTILATION, AND WHO ALSO KNEW WHY WE HAD COME TO AFRICA TO MAKE OUR FILM, HAD NONETHELESS PERMITTED HIS OWN DAUGHTERS TO BE MUTILATED. HIS EXCUSE: MUTILATION IS WOMEN'S BUSINESS. THE WIFE IS SCOTTISH. THE HUSBAND, GAMBIAN. THE CHILDREN WHO HAVE BEEN MUTILATED ARE BY HIS FIRST WIFE, A GAMBIAN WOMAN, FOR WHOM FEMALE GENITAL MUTILATION IS CUSTOM AND TRADITION. WHILE WE WERE FILMING IN THE GAMBIA WE TALKED AT LENGTH WITH THE SECOND WIFE WHO WAS WORRIED ABOUT THE FATE OF HER HUSBAND'S DAUGHTERS. SHE HAD BEEN WILLING TO HAVE THE GIRLS LIVE WITH HER AND HER HUSBAND, IN AN EFFORT TO SAVE THEM.

The sad thing is, I can understand our driver's sense of powerlessness as a man (in most African societies female genital mutilation is almost entirely in the hands of women). His first wife's sense of duty and tradition. His second wife's horror and disappointment. We are not talking about bad or evil people.

Far from it. They are, however, trapped in a behavior that severely harms them.

It is from the perspective of our own contradictions as a society that we must seek to comprehend this grave problem faced by millions of our planet's children and suffered by millions of our women. And suffered as well by men, who are by no means exempt from the self-inflicted wounding of the total society that mutilation ensures.

These mutilations of body and spirit have occurred for from three to six thousand years. It is likely that they will continue well into the future, no matter what we do. That is why I try to focus on one child or one woman, when I think of the struggle ahead, instead of on all the millions who are at risk.

In *Warrior Marks*, Pratibha Parmar and I are sending a message to our sisters, millions of them yet unborn—and to our brothers who love them—and the message is this: If in fact you survive your mutilation, and the degradation that it imprints on soul and body, you still have a life to live. Live it with passion, live it with fierceness, live it with all the joy and laughter you deserve.

Because your elders have told you you are unclean does not make it so.

Because your mother has told you must hang your head in sorrow because you were born female, does not make it so.

Because your father tells you he owns your body and soul and can do what he likes with you, does not make it so.

Because your religion tells you there is a God who demands pieces of your flesh, and your perpetual suffering in sex and childbearing, does not mean this is *your* religion or *your* God.

The earth and all its fullness, including your body, belongs to you. As does heaven itself. Whose other name is, of course, peace.

We know that women and children who suffer genital mutilation will have to stand up for themselves, and, together, put an end to it. But that they need our help is indisputable.

What we can do is say:

Out of our own suffering we can recognize yours.

Out of our own outrage, we join our voices to yours.

Out of our own self-respect, we affirm your right to be self-respecting, and free from unwanted invasion or attack.

What can *you* do?

You can refrain from spending more than ten minutes stoning or attempting to malign the messenger. Within those minutes thousands of children will be mutilated. Your idle words will have the rumble of muffled screams beneath them.

You can study the situation and be informed, so that when children are at risk in your own neighborhood, you will be aware of it. You can make every effort to remember that it is the act of genital mutilation we wish to get rid of, not the people, all of whom need our understanding and our love.

In that regard, I'd like to share the following story about my encounter with the circumciser/mutilator in the film. The most daunting thing about confronting evil is that it tires you, and on the day that I was to interview her I was feeling really terrible. I had seen the young girls shuffling back to the village after having been mutilated ten days before. I had seen their sadness, the lack of light in their eyes. I'd also noticed the arrogance of the circumciser/mutilator, as she sought to convey to us a sense of her own importance. When I asked her what she felt when she cut children and they screamed, and she said that she never heard them, I felt chilled, even in that very hot climate. Still, as we talked, and as I was compelled to confront her incredible denial of the pain she constantly inflicts, I found myself completely seeing the old woman before me. And when I did, when I recognized the limitations of her life, the choices thrust upon her by society, a society deadly to women; when I thought of her ignorance, deliberately enforced by the patriarchal intransigence of her culture, I felt all my anger, dread, and even my headache, draining away. I felt only compassion, which surprised me to no end, and also, in a sense, saved me.

In my fifty years among African Americans I've noticed that, because of our suffering and our centuries-long insecurity, we have a hard time believing we are lovable. We also have a great fear of learning "bad" things about ourselves because we are sure these "bad" things will be cause for more people not to love us. I learned this decisively when there was much controversy over my novel *The Color Purple*, and the subsequent film based on it. There were actually people who thought that because I exposed violence, incest, and rape within the black community, I hated black men. In a situation like that, as in this, there is a fear of being left behind, of being abandoned, of having no one on your side, if all this "stuff" is exposed. This feeling, which is very deep with us, is understandable: It is a legacy of our having been rejected, as human beings, by the Euro-Americans who enslaved us, and who set about undermining our language, our families, our bodily and mental integrity, and especially our sense of the sacred.

Today, however, it is precisely compassionate love of ourselves and of others in which we must have faith. I have learned nothing about human beings that has stopped my loving them, and this is especially true of African and African-American human beings, women and men, who seem to me unsurpassed inspirers of affection, wonder, and love.

A slightly modified version of these remarks was given before a screening of Warrior Marks *on February 24, 1994 in Oakland, California.*

ALICE WALKER is a prizewinning author whose numerous poetry collections and novels include *The Color Purple*, *Temple of My Familiar*, and *Possessing the Secret of Joy*. She contributed the foreword to Agnes Smedley's *Daughter of Earth* (The Feminist Press, 1987) and edited *I Love Myself When I Am Laughing…And Then Again When I Am Looking Mean and Impressive: A Zora Neale Hurston Reader* (The Feminist Press, 1979).

Photo by Jean Weisinger.

A Feminist in the Thirties —and Today

Margaret Walker

I GRADUATED FROM COLLEGE IN 1935. I WAS TWENTY YEARS OLD. ALL MY LIFE I HAVE DREAMED OF WRITING BOOKS AND HAVING THEM PUBLISHED. I PUBLISHED POETRY IN THREE MAGAZINES IN THE 1930s—*CRISIS* (1934), *OPPORTUNITY* (1938), AND *POETRY* (1937, 1938, 1939). I PUBLISHED PROSE ("THE RED SATIN DRESS") IN *CREATIVE WRITING* AND JACK CONROY'S *NEW ANVIL*. LOOKING BACK NOW OVER SIXTY YEARS AND KNOWING WHAT RACIAL AND GENDER PREJUDICE WAS LIKE IN THE 1930S, MY BEGINNINGS AS A PUBLISHED WRITER WERE NOT SO BAD. MY NEWEST BOOK, SCHEDULED FOR PUBLICATION IN 1995 IS *BEING FEMALE, BLACK, AND FREE.* I SAY *FREE* INSTEAD OF *POOR*.

Women's rights, civil rights, and human rights all mean the same thing to me. Four years after I was born the law allowed *white* women to vote. World War II first opened the doors of industry for women to work in defense. Women's rights for me means the right of a woman to make the same salary as a man for the same work. I taught school nearly forty years and my salary never equalled a man's with the same education, experience, or position. For fourteen of those forty years I was a full professor with book publications and a Ph.D. and I never made $25,000. My mother's mother was a fine seamstress but when the doctor ordered her outdoors away from her sewing machine she took in washing which paid $1.00 per week plus a grapefruit. When my mother was married a few years later, her first task was to take her mother out of the washtub.

One day reading the anthology *Writing Red*, which includes women writing in the thirties, I was amazed to discover that the black publications of the 1930s, where I published, were considered radical, militant, or red. I was never published in left-wing magazines, whether because of race or gender I do not know. But it interests me greatly to see black equated with red. Being a feminist in the 1930s, like the 1990s, means fighting for women's rights, for civil rights, for human rights—to change the world, to change society—to earn equal pay, to vote, to be elected to public office, to speak out and be heard.

One of our guests at Jackson State University was Bessie Head from Botswana and South Africa. I said to a male writer also from South Africa that I consider her one of the world's greatest novelists. He smiled and said, "Oh yes, she's a feminist." I looked at him in horror. What else could she be—female, black, and poor?

Recently, a black woman has won the Nobel Prize for literature. Three black women have won Pulitzer Prizes for literature. I cannot conceive of this happening in the 1930s. Perhaps the world is changing. Perhaps I hear a woman's strident voice.

MARGARET WALKER is professor emerita of English at Jackson State University. Her books include *For My People, Jubilee, Richard Wright: Daemonic Genius*, and *How I Wrote Jubilee and Other Essays on Life and Literature* (The Feminist Press, 1990).

Photo by David Rae Morris.

Rural Women

Carolyn Wedin

I HAVE LONG CARRIED A SIMPLE MENTAL MEASURING TOOL BY WHICH I GAUGE MY THOUGHTS ON THE ACCURACY, RELEVANCE, IMPORTANCE, AND INCLUSIVITY OF ANY MANIFESTO OF FEMINISM: IF IT DOES NOT INCLUDE THE LIVES OF WOMEN LIKE MY MOTHER, IT IS NOT BIG ENOUGH FOR ME.

Living from 1900 to 1984, my mother had only six years of schooling in one room in the northwest Wisconsin woods, but she self-directed her eight decades of education. Learning is not limited to school, she knew, especially when books and pencils and paper and eventually radios and TVs become accessible even in the most remote areas.

Married and giving birth to her first child at age sixteen, to be followed by eight others, the youngest, me, born when she was thirty-nine, my mother did not recognize maternal and paternal role divisions and limitations. On farms before electricity and tractors there was more than enough for everyone to do, much of it challenging physical labor. When mother and dad sit on adjoining milk stools, son and daughter see little reason why they should divide haying, cultivating, gardening, cooking, carpentering, sewing, or washing clothes along gender lines.

My parents lost their hard-worked, slowly built farm in the Great Depression, and I grew up on a diminished but cozy and secure piece of land and in a four-room house built of scraps. Hardship and dwindling means increased, not decreased, my mother's invention; my life in that small house was rich.

When I return to my early home, I see creative reflections of my mother kaleidoscoped in the lives of my sisters and nieces and childhood friends. When I read and write about U.S. literature I catch glimpses of her uncomplaining strengths in stories of immigration, of slavery, of both frontier and urban struggle.

Feminism must contain for me a philosophy and attitude toward learning which is not limited to the opportunities for schooling; a cooperative partnership across gender and generational lines which includes the necessity, the dignity, and the worth of physical labor; an assumption of life's challenges and constraints with creative ingenuity.

To recognize where these characteristics have been acted out in unheralded lives in our personal and national histories leads us organically to a wide-angled view of feminism's future around the world, particularly where the figurative seeds of change have their genesis in the literal seeds of sustenance flowing through women's hands.

Nature's abundance, variety, and inter-connectedness should be reflected, I believe, in the philosophies by which we human animals live and work in cooperation with nature. We are rooted and we are often transplanted; we make what we can of the soil which shields us; we bloom and we produce; we leave grains for future harvests.

CAROLYN WEDIN is professor of modern languages and literatures at the University of Wisconsin-Whitewater. She contributed the afterword to *Black and White Sat Down Together: Reminiscences of an NAACP Founder* by Mary White Ovington (The Feminist Press, 1995).

Photo by A. A. Rolloff

Mother's Day, 1990 *

Ingrid Wendt

AMONG SEVERAL MAJOR SHIFTS IN MY FEMINIST PERSPECTIVE OVER THE LAST TWENTY-FIVE YEARS, PERHAPS THE MOST VISIBLE IS MY ATTITUDE TOWARD THE TRADITIONAL ROLES OF WIFE, MOTHER, HOMEMAKER, CAREGIVER. NOT WANTING EVER TO BE LIKE MY MOTHER, NEWLY AWAKENED TO THE FACT THAT I DIDN'T *HAVE* TO BE, I USED TO RAIL AGAINST ALL THE VARIOUS FORMS OF DAILINESS THAT KEPT ME FROM MY ART, THAT KEPT OTHER WOMEN FROM BEING THEIR "TRUE" SELVES. NOW, IN RECENT YEARS, I FIND MYSELF

POSSESSED OF ANOTHER KIND OF FEROCITY: THE NEED TO CELEBRATE WHAT ALL AROUND ME I KEEP DISCOVERING IN UNEXPECTED QUARTERS: THE SMALL RITUALS OF DAILY LIVING—MANY OF THEM UNACKNOWLEDGED, NEARLY ALL UNDERVALUED—THAT REMIND US OF WHAT IT IS TO BE HUMAN, THAT GIVE US COURAGE AND STRENGTH AND AWARENESS OF WHAT IT IS WE FIGHT FOR, WHAT IT IS WE STAND FOR, AS WELL AS AGAINST, IN THESE TIMES OF UNPRECEDENTED GLOBAL PERIL.

As a testimony and example, I offer the following poem:

Next to me at the counter, a woman, a stranger
compliments our waiter on his tie.
Of course it could not go unnoticed: imperial
crests perched like red and black chickens
too big for the roost: out of place
among hashbrowns and toast as I was last night
reading mother and daughter poems to college students
in this high desert oasis where children are not
where it's at and mothers are who you have to
be seen with at breakfast during this annual visit

So why my surprise when the waiter suddenly beams,
becomes voluble; tells, although I can't hear, what is
surely his favorite tie story before moving on to refill my tea and
converse as though I were not old enough to be his own
mother: I, who at eighteen thought twenty-one unapproachable;
twenty-one, thought the faculty wife with toddlers already was over
the hill, had sold out; who just this morning, being seated,
has been looked through by just such another young woman,
her eyes on a future vague as glamour surely lying beyond
this tedium of courtesy, beyond this plain, blatant day.

And why am I suddenly grateful, as I found myself just
last week in the store when a clerk I'd never met exclaimed,
What a beautiful jacket! and I saw she was talking to me.
And why, less than an hour ago, asking directions of the older-
than-middle-aged filling station attendant, didn't I follow
my impulse to ask where she got that peach-colored orchid on
her lapel, so she could maybe have told me one of her children
gave it to her; so she could have someone to tell? Such

simple things, really: those moments of pleasure I keep learning
are *yes,* each day in our power to give each other, to help
keep this inescapable human circle in repair, keeping
each of us, as the lucky among us once were kept in the eyes
of our own mothers, visible. Whole.

*This poem first appeared in Fireweed, *Vol. 2, No. 3*

INGRID WENDT is the author of two books of poems, *Moving the House* and *Singing the Mozart Requiem*, which won the 1988 Oregon Book Award for Poetry. She coedited with Elaine Hedges *In Her Own Image: Women Working in the Arts* (The Feminist Press, 1980).

On Feminism

Wakako Yamauchi

WHAT DO I KNOW ABOUT FEMINISM? I WAS BORN TO JAPANESE IMMIGRANTS DURING THE GREAT DEPRESSION IN THE YEAR THE U.S. PASSED THE ASIAN EXCLUSION ACT. RACISM WAS EPIDEMIC THEN, AS IT USUALLY IS DURING ECONOMIC CRISIS. PRIMARY CONCERNS WERE PHYSICAL AND EMOTIONAL SURVIVAL; RACISM WAS DEALT WITH INDIVIDUALLY AS IT HAPPENED OR SIMPLY TOLERATED. SEXISM WAS A UNIVERSAL GIVEN. IT WAS RAMPANT IN OUR HOMES AS WELL AS IN THE LARGER SOCIETY. WE EITHER ACCEPTED IT AND SPENT THE ENERGY ON MORE PRESSING PROBLEMS OR FOUGHT IT BY SUBTERFUGE.

For generations Japanese women passed lessons of survival from mother to daughter through subtle (and not so subtle) signals: nudges, flashing glances, slowly closing eyes, and a pinch now and then. We were not supposed to talk too loud or to show excessive pain or exuberance. We avoided confrontation and abuse by giving ground, giving ground. It was called *makete katsu*—to win through losing. Those of us who found this too hard to do had a long row to hoe and were often ostracized or betrayed by our own. Still, when I saw my father and brother working in the fields like beasts of burden or watched them repair incomprehensible machinery or protect the family in dire catastrophe, I was glad to be a girl.

Like many rural families we were quite isolated. We had neither radio nor refrigerator until Secretary of Interior Harold Ickes sent electricity to the rural Imperial Valley. We rarely went to movies and we did not subscribe to American newspapers. We were politically and socially naive. My father, however, bought subscriptions to women's magazines (his way of getting rid of traveling salesmen) and I was greatly influenced by the articles and ads in them. I grew up thinking American women were mostly concerned with romance, cooking, clothes, and controlling bad breath, underarm and body odor. Poverty, racism, and sexism did not exist for them. What a life!

That was then. The world since has become more aware of ethnic and sexual diversity and the need for personal liberation. Women are everywhere men are and the division of labor is no longer clear-cut. We cannot always be nurturers while also working as hunters and gatherers. We cannot always be gentle and beguiling while striking out against inequities. We are understanding more about ourselves and we are becoming real people.

But centuries of indoctrination aren't overcome in a few generations. As we learn more, we will inform our sons and daughters and all will take responsibility for the work that must be done to make life more comfortable, more equitable, more loving for everyone.

WAKAKO YAMAUCHI has been writing for over thirty years and is best known for her play *And the Soul Shall Dance*, which was filmed by PBS. She is winner of the 1994 Lila Wallace-Reader's Digest Writers' Award and author of *Songs My Mother Taught Me: Stories, Plays*, and *Memoir* (The Feminist Press, 1994).

A Space for Difference

Jean Fagan Yellin

WHAT WAS IT LIKE A QUARTER OF A CENTURY AGO, BEFORE THE FEMINIST PRESS WAS ESTABLISHED? TYPING ON STENCILS THE TEXTS I THOUGHT I NEEDED FOR MY STUDENTS AND THEN RUNNING THEM OFF ON A DITTO MACHINE WAS LONELY, FRUSTRATING WORK. IT WAS LONELY AND FRUSTRATING TO BELIEVE THAT NO ONE ELSE WAS STRUGGLING TO FIND THESE TEXTS, THAT NO ONE ELSE WAS INTERESTED IN THE DIFFICULT NEW IDEAS THAT BOTH FRIGHTENED AND EXCITED ME. IT WAS LONELY AND FRUSTRATING TO BELIEVE THAT NEITHER ACADEMIC NOR TRADE PRESSES WERE PARTICULARLY INTERESTED IN PUBLISHING WHAT I THOUGHT ABOUT THOSE IDEAS, IN THOSE DAYS WHEN I WONDERED IF I EVER WOULD MANAGE TO SORT OUT MY THOUGHTS.

Now the books on my reading lists and syllabi—as well as the books on my bedtable—testify to the fruitful role of The Feminist Press. While its presence has spurred other presses to feature titles appropriate for "Gender Studies," The Feminist Press still has a pioneering role to play. Ideas about the category "woman" continue to develop. In light of the differences among us today—of class, of race, of nationality, of culture, of ethnicity, of age—feminists like myself urgently need a place where we can begin to confront our differences. It is not easy, when we know ourselves as oppressed, to see ourselves as oppressors in the eyes of our sisters. And this unease, I think, suggests the important role of The Feminist Press today. It is, perhaps, a space where we can begin to talk about the complicated intersections of gender with class, race, nationality, culture, ethnicity, and age. This conversation will not ever be easy and will perhaps at times not even be civil. But it is, I think, the task before us now.

JEAN FAGAN YELLIN is Distinguished Professor of English at Pace University. She contributed the afterword to *Margret Howth*, a novel by Rebecca Harding Davis (The Feminist Press, 1990).

I Believe

Amy Zerner

I BELIEVE THAT FOR MOST OF THE WOMEN IN THE WORLD, CONDITIONS ARE NOT MUCH BETTER THAN THEY WERE DURING THE DARK AGES, BUT:

I believe in a world where women speak their minds, don't second-guess themselves, and are powerful enough to rid themselves of the demon voices that tell them they are not good enough.

I believe in a world where we have regained our link to the Goddess force that is the fighter for truth and justice, as well as the giver of life, wisdom, intuition, and healing.

I believe in a world where spirituality is not mocked, but is recognized as the remembrance that all that we create begins within our mind, and that our hearts are our antennae toward the future.

I believe in a world where we nurture and develop our inner selves so as to be confident and clear of negative programming.

I believe in a world where we do not judge our outer selves except with forgiveness, compassion, and a sense of humor.

I believe in a world where we don't have to be "nice girls," because that's not nice.

I believe in a world where men are feminists.

I believe in a world where visions and re-visions are expected and respected.

I believe I am working to create the new and better world I believe in, and that you are, too.

To Be Myself

Jessie Spicer Zerner

WHEN I LOOK BACK ON MY EARLY LIFE IT SEEMS TO BE BASED ON CHARACTERS IN MOVIES RATHER VAGUELY REALIZED AND EASILY DISCARDED IF INAPPROPRIATE. I SMOKED CIGARETTES LIKE BETTE DAVIS AND TRIED TO BE AS FUNNY AND CHARMING AS KATHERINE HEPBURN. WHEN I MARRIED, I SLID QUICKLY INTO THE HOMEMAKER ROLE RATHER MORE INFLUENCED BY ADVERTISING THAN THE CINEMA.

Everything was made from scratch. Picture windows were washed twice a month. Brownies, Girl Scouts, Cub Scouts, the 4-H Club and the PTA were all part of my existence. Since I was also a commercial artist, someone was always asking me to make posters. You name it, I made a poster for it.

This, in my case, was not entirely the work of society, except in a very abstract sense, nor of my mother who was a buyer for Sloan's, a large New York furniture store, and who did none of those things. My husband was undemanding and not particularly conventional. Somehow, as the only child of an artist couple, I didn't have a clue as how to act in the world in which I discovered myself. We moved quite often and I had few close friends for any length of time or other families to learn from.

My children, of course, became my teachers in the end. They went to college. They talked about "women's lib." When my husband died at far too young an age, I had to find out how to read a bus schedule, how to live by myself and, more importantly, to be myself. In all the busy work with which I had filled my life, I had had no chance to discover me.

The main thing that surprises me about life when you look back is that it is always changing and renewing itself and that you can change, too. It isn't always easy but it's wonderful and someday, as I did, you may sit down beside a new role model at the hairdresser's, have her smile at you, and realize that she is Betty Friedan. I've come a long way.

AMY ZERNER (left) is an NEA awardee and illustrator and creator of *The Enchanted Tarot*, *The Alchemist*, and *Goddess, Guide Me*. She created the cover for *The Mer-Child: A Legend for Children and Other Adults* by Robin Morgan (The Feminist Press, 1991). JESSIE SPICER ZERNER has written and illustrated hundreds of children's books, and contributed illustrations to the *The Mer-Child*. The Zerners' other collaborative efforts have included *Zen ABC*, *Scheherazade's Cat*, and *The Dream Quilt*.

Photo by Gary Bartoloni.

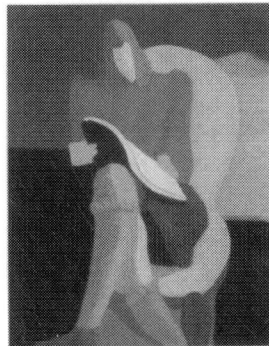

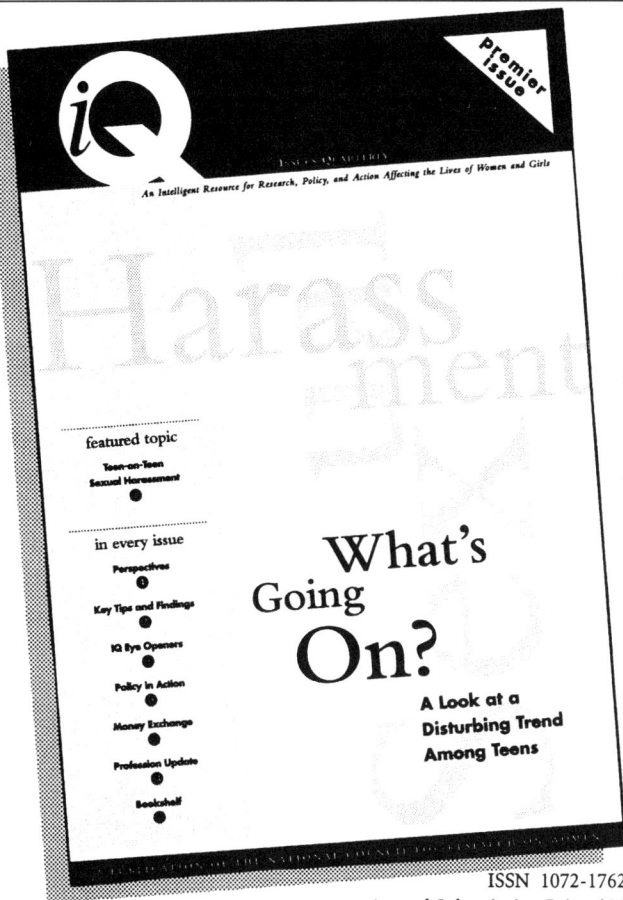

The best selling feminist magazine in the world.

LANI GUINIER The Untold Story

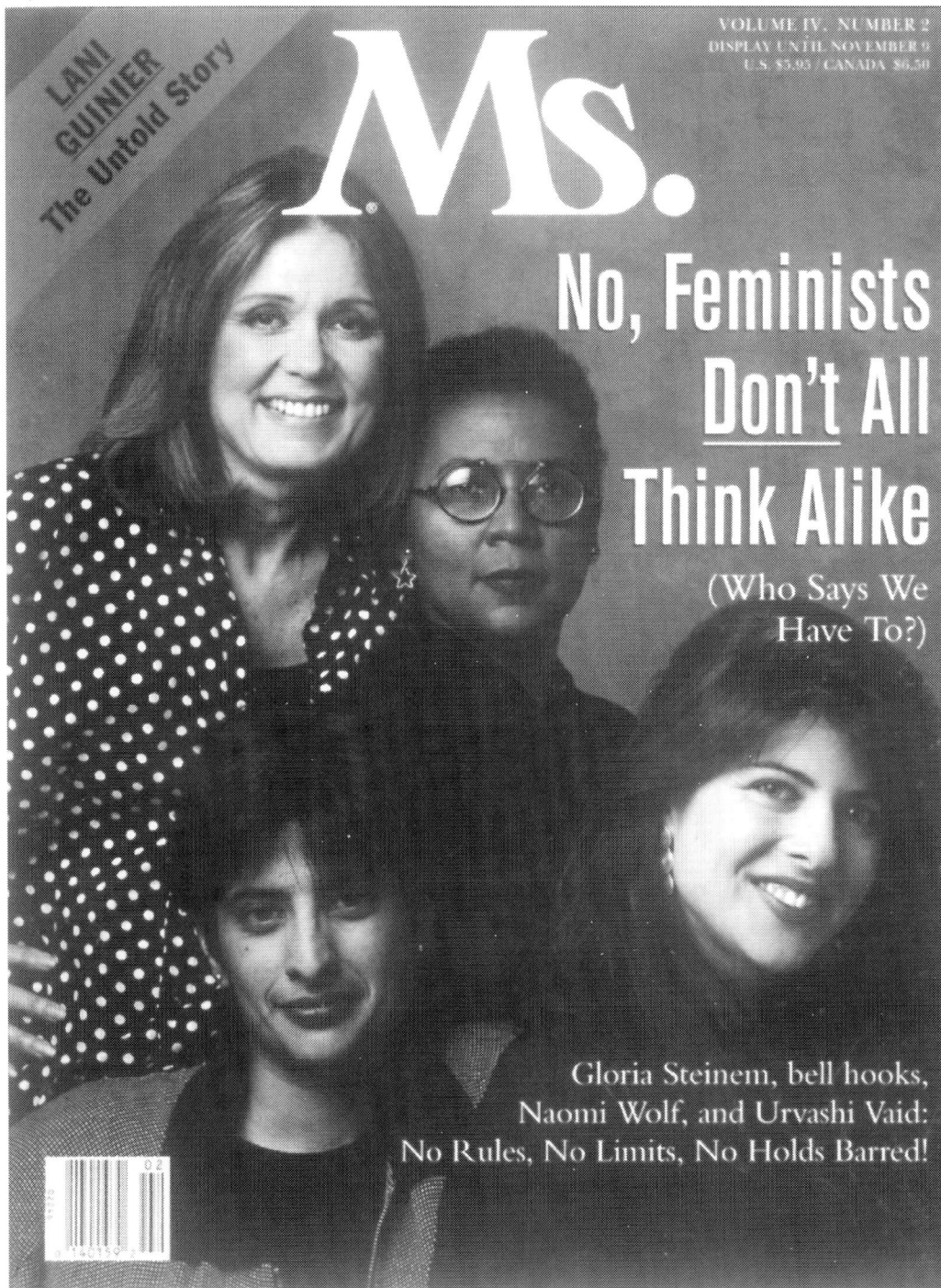

VOLUME IV, NUMBER 2
DISPLAY UNTIL NOVEMBER 9
U.S. $5.95 / CANADA $6.50

Ms.

No, Feminists Don't All Think Alike

(Who Says We Have To?)

Gloria Steinem, bell hooks, Naomi Wolf, and Urvashi Vaid: No Rules, No Limits, No Holds Barred!

Gertrude Stein Remembered

Edited by Linda Simon
A collection of memoirs by twenty people who knew her well, it adds invaluable details to our view of Stein as a writer and woman. $20 cloth

Mass Rape

The War against Women in Bosnia-Herzegovina
Edited by Alexandra Stiglmayer
Translated by Marion Faber
Foreword by Roy Gutman
Afterword by Cynthia Enloe
This first English edition includes interviews with some twenty victims of rape as well as interviews with three Serbian perpetrators. $14.95 paper, $35 cloth

Second to None

A Documentary History of American Women
Volume I: From the Sixteenth Century to 1865
Volume II: From 1865 to the Present
Edited by Ruth Barnes Moynihan, Cynthia Russett, and Laurie Crumpacker
"A superb collection. The editors have amassed an unusually wide-ranging set of documents. . . . extremely strong and valuable. I recommend it."—Sarah J. Deutsch
Vol. I: $20 paper, $45 cloth / Vol. II: $20 paper, $45 cloth

The Hart Sisters

Early African Caribbean Writers, Evangelicals, and Radicals
Edited and with an introduction by Moira Ferguson
These members of the "free colored" community who married white men and played an active role as educators, antislavery activists, and Methodist evangelicals were also among the first African Caribbean female writers. This exceptional volume offers for the first time a collection of their writings. $40 cloth

Constructive Criticism:

Columbia Builds on 100 Years of Excellence

Precarious Dependencies
GENDER, CLASS, AND DOMESTIC SERVICE IN BOLIVIA
Lesley Gill
208 pp / $16.00 paper / $45.00 cloth
Through oral histories, court cases, and field-work interviews, Gill examines the mistress-servant relationship in Bolivia between 1930 and 1990, asking how gender and ethnicity are mediated by class position and historical experience, and how changing power relations have both sustained and altered social, cultural, and ethnic distinctions.

Fruit of the Motherland
GENDER IN AN EGALITARIAN SOCIETY
Maria Lepowsky
344 pp / 20 photos / $17.50 paper / $49.00 cloth
Lepowsky's study of the Vanatinai in New Guinea reveals a matrilineal, decentralized society where there is no ideology of male dominance and women and men are considered fundamentally equal.
"A very interesting and important study....Very well written, with an easy style."
—Jane Goodale, Bryn Mawr College

With a new introduction...
Factory Women in Taiwan
Lydia Kung
288 pp / $16.00 paper / $39.00 cloth
Describing the first generation of Taiwanese working women, Kung addresses the effects of wage-earning on their status and lives, especially on the parent-daughter relationship. She demonstrates that factory work becomes a new opportunity to meet already existing role expectations, and that the values on which these roles are based have not changed.

Women and Words in Saudi Arabia
THE POLITICS OF LITERARY DISCOURSE
Saddeka Arebi
320 pp / $17.50 paper / $49.50 cloth
Demonstrating that contemporary Saudi women writers use their work as a way to gain control over the rules of cultural discourse in their society, Arebi analyzes the work of nine of the most influential women writers, presenting excerpts of their writings which appear here for the first time in English.

New in paper...
An Ordered Society
GENDER AND CLASS IN EARLY MODERN ENGLAND
Susan Dwyer Amussen
216 pp / $16.00 paper
Amussen's vivid account of family and village life in England, from the reign of Elizabeth I to the accession of the Hanoverian monarchies, describes the domestic economy of the rich and poor; the processes of courtship, marriage, and marital breakdown; and the structure of power within the family and in rural communities. She analyzes two separate systems of social hierarchy—class and gender—which were often in conflict.

New in paper...with a new preface
Becoming A Heroine
READING ABOUT WOMEN IN NOVELS
Rachel M. Brownstein
360 pp / $14.95 paper
"A splendid book, a rare combination of critical brilliance and personal warmth. Brownstein speaks for a generation, perhaps a tradition, of passionate women readers; she stands for literary values that need to be defended against the chilling abstractions of contemporary theory, and that remind us why we read and how we shape our lives by our books."
—Elaine Showalter

New in paper...
Unbecoming Women
BRITISH WOMEN WRITERS AND THE NOVEL OF DEVELOPMENT
Susan Fraiman
192 pp / $15.00 paper
"Fraiman's argument is thoroughly researched and carefully detailed. She particularly excels at laying bare the hidden gender and class dynamics prompting the demands of structure, of locating narrative questions within a critical tradition and theory."
—Laurie Langbauer, Swarthmore College

Revised Edition
Recovery
HOW TO SURVIVE SEXUAL ASSAULT FOR WOMEN, MEN, TEENAGERS, AND THEIR FRIENDS AND FAMILY
Helen Benedict with a new Foreword by Susan Brison
352 pp / $14.95 paper / $29.95 cloth
"Benedict's book—practical, pointed, comprehensive, and accessible—should be read by everyone above the age of 10 for its compassionate, direct, and most clear advice to the sexually assaulted and all those close to them. It deserves special applause for focusing on rape victims generally ignored in other studies: lesbians, the elderly, teenagers of both sexes, gay and straight men, the disabled and incest survivors."
—Ms. Magazine

Wild Desires and Mistaken Identities
LESBIANISM AND PSYCHOANALYSIS
Noreen O'Connor and Joanna Ryan
315 pp / $30.00 cloth
Based on the authors' clinical experience as psychoanalytic psychotherapists, this reconsideration of lesbian lives and lesbian experiences offers a new and thoughtful framework that does not inevitably pathologize or universalize all lesbianism; instead, it argues for the development of a theory and practice open to the complexities of individual life histories, relationships, and identities.

The Lesbian Postmodern
Edited by Laura Doan
268 pp / $16.50 paper / $49.50 cloth
"As an exploration of the relation between the lesbian, conceived within the context of cutting edge work on gender theory, and postmodernism, a term also requiring critical scrutiny, these essays generate a rich and complex arena for the study of both terms."
—Elizabeth Meese, University of Alabama

BUILDING ON 100 YEARS OF EXCELLENCE

COLUMBIA UNIVERSITY PRESS
SINCE 1893

CREDIT CARDS ACCEPTED.
DEPT. S72 / 136 SOUTH BROADWAY / IRVINGTON / NY 10533 / TEL (800) 944-8648 / FAX (800) 944-1844
CALL OR WRITE FOR OUR COMPLETE CATALOG.

Brooklyn College President
Vernon E. Lattin

and

The Brooklyn College Community
Join in Celebrating the 20th Anniversary
of the
Brooklyn College Women's Studies
Program
and
Women's Center

SPELMAN COLLEGE

For a quarter of a century,
the Feminist Press
has brought us the voices of
diverse women of the world.
In sisterhood, the Spelman
College Family expresses
gratitude and hearty
congratulations for this work
well done.

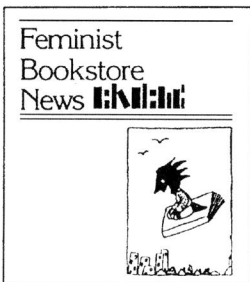

*The Board of Directors
of The Feminist Press at CUNY*
*would like to thank our readers, authors, and supporters
for keeping The Feminist Press at the forefront
of feminist publishing for the past twenty-five years.*

•

WITHOUT YOU, THERE WOULD BE NO FEMINIST PRESS!

With your continued support, we hope to serve you for
twenty-five more years—and beyond.